African
INTELLECTUALS
in 19th and early 20th century
SOUTH AFRICA

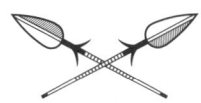

African INTELLECTUALS
in 19th and early 20th century
SOUTH AFRICA

Edited by Mcebisi Ndletyana

Commissioned and funded by the Amathole District Municipality (East London) and the National Heritage Commission. Compiled within the Democracy and Governance Research Programme of the Human Sciences Research Council

Published by HSRC Press
Private Bag X9182, Cape Town, 8000, South Africa
www.hsrcpress.ac.za

First published 2008

ISBN 978-0-7969-2207-6

© 2008 Human Sciences Research Council

The views expressed in this publication are those of the authors. They do not necessarily reflect the views or policies of the Human Sciences Research Council ('the Council') or indicate that the Council endorses the views of the authors. In quoting from this publication, readers are advised to attribute the source of the information to the individual author concerned and not to the Council.

Copyedited by Angela Briggs
Typeset by Simon van Gend
Cover design by FUEL
Print management by comPress

Distributed in Africa by Blue Weaver
Tel: +27 (0) 21 701 4477; Fax: +27 (0) 21 701 7302
www.oneworldbooks.com

Distributed in Europe and the United Kingdom by Eurospan Distribution Services
Tel: +44 (0) 20 7240 0856; Fax: +44 (0) 20 7379 0609
www.eurospangroup.com/bookstore

Distributed in North America by Independent Publishers Group (IPG)
Call toll-free: (800) 888 4741; Fax: +1 (312) 337 5985
www.ipgbook.com

Printed by Creda Communications

Contents

Foreword　*vii*

Acknowledgements　*x*

1. INTRODUCTION　1
   Mcebisi Ndletyana

2. NTSIKANA　7
   Vuyani Booi

3. TIYO SOGA　17
   Mcebisi Ndletyana

4. JOHN TENGO JABAVU　31
   Mcebisi Ndletyana

5. MPILO WALTER BENSON RUBUSANA　45
   Songezo Joel Ngqongqo

6. SAMUEL EDWARD KRUNE MQHAYI　55
   Mncedisi Qangule

Notes　*67*

Picture credits　*71*

Contributors　*73*

References　*75*

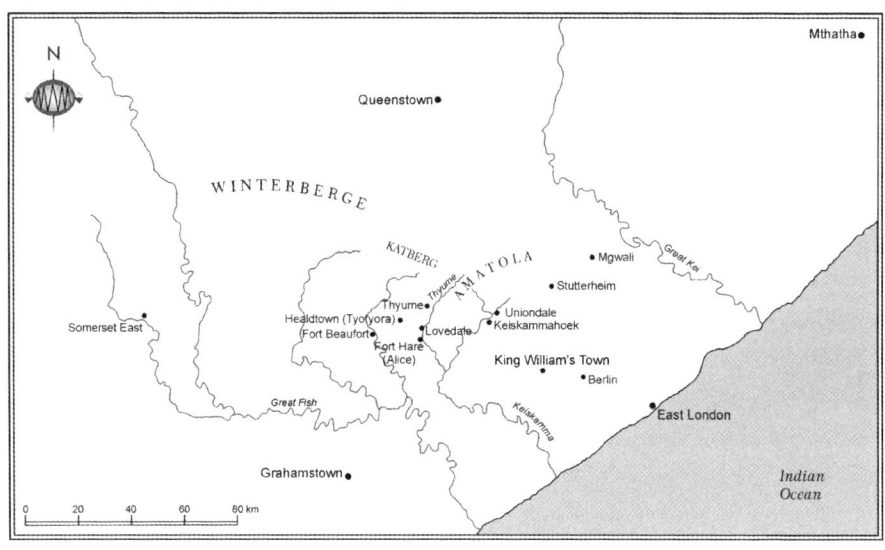

Part of the Eastern Cape, showing the home to Ntsikana, Tiyo Soga, John Tengo Jabavu, Mpilo Walter Benson Rubusana and Samuel Edward Krune Mqhayi.

The 1998 Nobel Prize Laureate for Economics, Amartya Sen, has written a very enlightening and engaging book on contemporary India, *The Argumentative Indian: Writings on Indian Culture, History and Identity* (2005). This book of essays is enlightening because it seeks to situate contemporary India, its culture, politics and aspirations, within the context of an ancient historical tradition of diversity and heterodoxy. For this he draws from and reinterprets India's literary traditions, philosophy, culture and religions, so as to understand and distinguish claims to authenticity and indigeneity within societies that have long intermingled and been affected by a diversity of influences. Likewise, the essays are engaging because they take issue with many of the truth claims in contemporary Indian politics about secularism and Hindu nationalism, they revisit ancient Sanskrit and Hindi texts, and they offer refreshing interpretations that are sure to make many fundamentalists uneasy and unsure.

This recovery of ancient wisdom is an exercise in the recovery of intellectual traditions as a tool to a better understanding of contemporary society. Such an exercise is equally valuable in South Africa. It is important if we are to understand the roots of debate and engagement, and the world of ideas and the influences which shaped the thinking of African men and women of ideas in the nineteenth and early twentieth centuries. It requires of us a very rigorous re-examination of the claims that are being made in today's politics, culture, philosophy and religion. It establishes the value of an intellectual tradition that is rooted in the cultures and common wisdom of the people, and yet is influenced by the cultures of the settler communities without the loss of language and traditions. Sen uses the laconic expression that 'voice is a crucial component of the pursuit of justice'. That suggests to me that during times of oppression or national crisis (which marked much of the nineteenth century), the poets, preachers and writers gave voice to the silent. Elsewhere he recalls a visit to his native Bengali village. An old man who was very poor and most probably illiterate commented in conversation with the famous laureate, 'It is not very hard to silence us, but that is not because we cannot speak'. African societies in colonial South Africa reflected their own elements of the Enlightenment, the tradition of dialogue, the 'argumentative' part of Sen's title. The critical voices that expressed the minds of those deprived of voice by reason of their status in life and the opportunities that passed them by, and the pride of language and culture that was the mainstay of their identity and human aspirations are embodied in the personalities whose characters are sketched in this volume. They represent a few of the well-known intellectuals of their time, literary geniuses and social commentators who transcended both their own cultures and the confines of the mind that missionary education and religion sought to impose on them.

The benefit of these studies is that they give insight into a period in our country which has been all but lost through the intervening 50 years of apartheid rule, and through the quislingite re-interpretations of Bantustan control mechanisms. Even more important, the intellectual traditions represented here, far from being uniform, expose the heterodoxy of those early intellectuals in our country. Nor is this an exercise in showing a bias towards the Eastern Cape in the understanding of this country's intellectual tradition. In looking to the roots and sources of the liberation tradition long before the ANC's inception in 1912, it demonstrates that beyond the confines of the geo-political peculiarities of colonial boundaries and Boer republics, black South Africans had begun to speak a common language and shared a common

FOREWORD

aspiration. Beyond the intellectual acuity revealed in these studies, we have a study in social and political leadership worthy of emulation during our trying times.

This is deliberately set as a popular reader in order to make these giants of the intellectual tradition of the nineteenth and early twentieth centuries available to ordinary South Africans, especially the younger generation. The Human Sciences Research Council, the National Heritage Council, and the Amathole District Municipality (East London) are to be commended on this timely publication.

Professor N Barney Pityana
Vice-Chancellor and Principal, University of South Africa

This book is timely and its value is timeless. The literature on South Africa's first native encounters with Europeans, particularly resistance against colonial dispossession, often depicts one dimension of Africans – the warrior tradition. These early encounters are often narrated by colonialists or early missionaries, the very same individuals whose mission was to convert natives into their own subjects, thereby moulding them into their own image. Such literature has always posed a dilemma as it is inherently biased when told from one side of the conflict.

Yet, material collected from oral tradition or orature tends to be complex. Sometimes it is figurative rather than factual and thus suffers from distortions over time. What has always been lacking is the African voice that reflects on how Africans experienced and interpreted the early encounters with Europeans. The works and social histories of the early modern African intellectuals have the greatest potential of closing this yawning gap, and this book is a major contribution in this regard.

This slim volume gives a voice to Africans in a manner that makes us understand how they interpreted and reacted to colonial conquest and the missionary proselytising project. It also reveals an intricate and complex process in which these public intellectuals had to straddle both the Western and the African worlds in which they were grounded or exposed. It is this interplay between tradition and modernity within the social, political, religious and economic spaces of these scholars that makes it valuable.

The National Heritage Council of South Africa has the specific mandate of transforming the heritage landscape of South Africa by, among other things, mainstreaming the living, or 'intangible', heritage which has always been marginalised or subverted. This volume is a product of many role-players who collaborated in supporting its successful execution and completion. The National Heritage Council, Human Sciences Research Council, Amathole District Municipality and Fort Hare University worked together to provide both intellectual and financial resources. This partnership of a heritage institution, a municipality, a research institution and an institution of higher learning is a model that can be used by others when faced with such a complex project with limited resources.

It is hoped that this pilot project, which focuses on the Eastern Cape, will be extended to other parts of the country in order to give witness to the role of public intellectuals who, in many ways, formed the foundation of the modern nationalist liberation struggle against colonialism and apartheid.

We have to commend the intellectual leadership provided by Dr Mcebisi Ndletyana, who was the project leader and manager of the project. Dr Xolela Mangcu deserves our gratitude for the formative role he played in the conceptual stage of this book. Our special appreciation goes to each of the authors – Ndletyana, Mncedisi Qangule, Vuyani Booi and Songezo Joel Ngqongqo – for their dedication and commitment to producing this volume. Luvuyo Dondolo from the Amathole District Municipality, especially, deserves a special mention for the important role he played in the evolution and completion of this book. East London's Amathole District Municipality has played a pioneering role in many heritage-related initiatives, notably the Eastern Cape heritage trail.

National Heritage Council, South Africa

1
INTRODUCTION

Mcebisi Ndletyana

This slim volume profiles the lives and works of five individuals: Ntsikana, Tiyo Soga, John Tengo Jabavu, Mpilo Walter Benson Rubusana and Samuel Edward Krune Mqhayi. These individuals played a pioneering role in the evolution of intellectual activity among Africans in the nineteenth century. They distinguished themselves in their various fields, rising to become the most influential of the early African intellectuals in South Africa.

We take our definition of an intellectual from the Italian scholar Antonio Gramsci. Intellectuals are individuals who, by virtue of their position in society and intellectual training, are preoccupied with abstract ideas, not only for self-gratification, but also to fulfill a public role. Intellectuals explain new experiences and ideas in the most accessible and understandable ways to the rest of society. This is particularly so in a society that is undergoing a transition, where people are grappling with and seeking to make sense of the new and unknown world. Intellectuals thus provide answers and leadership mainly in the conception and articulation of ideas.

These early intellectuals, based in the Cape, owe their rise to the cumulative impact of missionary activities, as well as to British colonialism. Missionaries first arrived among Xhosas in September 1799. The pioneer of this evangelical mission was Johannes van der Kemp (known as '*Nyengana*' – one who comes secretly – among locals), a medical doctor and scholar from the London Missionary Society. Fifty years later, eleven missionary societies, with a total of no fewer than 150 personnel, had established themselves on South African soil. By the formation of the Union, in 1910, the number of priests stood at 2 000, and the number of missionary societies had jumped to more than thirty.

Missionaries used education and literature to spread the gospel: education enabled potential converts to read the Bible. For this reason, mission stations were centres of learning. The most prominent mission station was Lovedale, founded in 1820, in Alice. Lovedale counted priests and teachers, who were subsequently employed to 'save more souls', among its graduates. They spread literacy and Christianity among fellow Xhosas.

The Bible and newspapers were the most common pieces of literature among the indigenous Xhosa population at that time. Literary work itself was first initiated in 1824, with the production of a small spelling-book published at the Chumie (Thyume) Mission Press. The first newspaper, *Umshumayeli Wendaba* (*The Publisher of News*), was launched in July 1837. Though lasting for only four years (closing in April 1841), *Umshumayeli* produced 15 editions at three-month intervals and was a pioneer of newspapers among the indigenous population. It was followed by many other publications: *Isibuto Samavo* (*A Collection of Stories*) in 1843; *Ikwezi* (*The Morning Star*) in August 1844; *Isitunywa Senyanga* (*The Monthly Messenger*) in August 1850; *Indaba* (*The News*) in 1861; and *Isigidimi Sama-Xosa* (*The Xhosa Express*, later changed to *Christian Express*, then to *South African Outlook*) followed in 1881. The 1880s saw the launch of the first ever non-missionary newspaper, *Imvo Zabantsundu* (*Native Opinion*), and was followed by yet another milestone in 1897, the founding of the first independent African newspaper, *Izwi Labantu* (*The Voice of the People*). The early newspapers enjoyed a relatively brief lifespan due mainly to military turbulence on the frontier and lack of a wide and consistent readership. Only three African-focused newspapers in the Cape survived into the twentieth century: *Imvo*, *Izwi* and *Christian Express*.

Education among Africans received a colonial boost from 1854 onwards. The colonial state undertook to 'subsidise missionary institutions that would undertake to train Bantu youth in industrial occupation and to fit them to act as interpreters, evangelists and school masters among their own people'. New schools were built, including Healdtown, St Matthew's, St Mark's, Salem, Peelton, and Mount Coke, among others. Facilities such as Lovedale were improved. African enrolment in government aided schools rose to 49 555 by 1887. Between 1874 and 1904, 1 502 teachers were trained at various training schools and by 1887 more than 2 000 pupils had received secondary education at Lovedale alone. Other high school graduates went on to become religious ministers, journalists, labour agents, legal assistants and interpreters.

These post-1854 'civilising' initiatives were a result of a policy shift within the colonial administration to pursue a 'policy of civilisation'. The British had colonised the Cape in 1806, but official opinion was divided over whether to place the locals under British rule, or let them be. Needless to say, disagreement over policy did not render territorial conquest unimportant. The British expanded their colonial territory by dispossessing Xhosas through repeated wars. By 1850, colonial boundaries had been extended from the eastern bank of the Fish River, where boer-trekkers had co-habited with the Xhosas since 1811, to the Kei River. The very first inter-racial contact between Xhosas and boer-trekkers had occurred in 1702 around the Fish River, fifty years after Dutch settlers had first docked their ships on the Cape shores.

The civilising policy owed much to the Victorian convictions of its colonial administrator, Sir George Grey. He believed that 'the natives' were not intellectually inferior to the rest of the human race and thus could be easily civilised. And this, Grey believed, could be achieved through the imposition of British law, education, and conversion to wage labour, and through colonial settlement among the 'natives'. The law and education would instill civilised values, while wage labour would nurture ambition for material improvement. Colonial settlers would serve as an example of civilised character as well as provide further employment on their farms. Christianised and civilised,

Grey believed, the Xhosa would cease being a British foe, and become a friend. Peace would eventually prevail in the frontier. And after the catastrophic effects of the 1855/56 cattle killing and destruction of crops, as Xhosas complied with the Nongqawuse prophecy, the Xhosa did become notably vulnerable to colonial influence. An estimated 30 000 left their homes for the colony in search of employment.

Thus the colonial state and the missionary enterprise shared a common objective: to create an indigenous middle class that would share similar value systems and economic interests to the settler community. This middle class would, in turn, be protective of the colonial society, serve as a pacifier of the Xhosa community, and help to spread 'civilisation'. The doyen of South African missionaries, John Phillip, emphasised the link in 1820:

> Tribes in a savage state are generally without houses, gardens, and fixed property. By locating them on a particular place, getting them to build houses, enclose gardens, cultivate corn land, accumulate property, and by increasing their artificial wants, you increase their dependency on the colony, and multiply the bonds of union and the number of securities for the preservation of peace.

Peasantry provided another route towards middle-class status. Missions not only provided teaching on farming, but also land on which to farm. Missionaries had access to vast tracts of land. By 1848, for instance, the colonial administration had issued 70 000 acres of land to mission stations, while another 155 000 acres was held by virtue of tickets of occupation. Individuals could lease mission land and generate income for themselves and to pay rent and taxes.

The civilising mission also decreed that the franchise be open to all males regardless of race, subject to property and income qualifications. Voting was done by word of mouth. To qualify, one needed property worth twenty-five pounds, or to receive an annual salary of fifty pounds. One also had to be a natural-born British subject. This meant only the Mfengus, among the Xhosa, were eligible for the franchise. Others became eligible later, notably from 1879 onwards, as more 'native territories' fell to Britain. The Xhosa vote became a decisive one in some constituencies. Some English-speaking liberal politicians, for instance, owed their election to Nguni voters.

In short, early African intellectuals were a product of the missionary enterprise and the British civilising mission. They were part of a new middle class that the colonial agents wanted as a buffer between colonial society and the rest of the indigenous population. Members of this middle class were also intended to become agents of the civilising mission themselves. They were Christian converts (and later priests), and graduates of missionary schools. Many of them went on to play leading roles in the various aspects of the emerging modern society.

Beneficiaries of the civilising mission they were, yet they refused to define themselves in the image of their colonial benefactors. Rather, they re-defined themselves, combining the best of the two worlds into what became a modern African identity and a unique contribution to South African modernity.

Popular recollection of the history of Africans often centres on colonial conquest, and recalls Africans solely as recipients of modernity. Yet, early converts were more than just recipients, but went on to become co-architects of South African modernity in their own right. In the area of Christianity, which was embryonic in early nineteenth century South Africa, Ntsikana made a pioneering contribution to hymn-writing in Xhosa, and combined Christianity with the indigenous value system. He demonstrated, as is now a commonplace, that one could be Christian while also adhering to one's own value system. The two were not mutually exclusive. Soga counselled pride in African history, and spoke of African ability at the height of colonial racism in the 1850s. His views laid the basis for the genesis of the black consciousness movement more than a century later. Jabavu initiated black newspapers and popularised the culture of reading within the black community, not only for its intrinsic value but also to promote popular participation in the political process. If Jabavu encouraged reading within the African community, Mqhayi pioneered African literature.

And Rubusana advocated for an idea that is only now gaining real traction within the education sector – mother-tongue instruction.

We trust that this volume whets your appetite for more information about early African intellectuals, and stimulates much further research into their lives – and the lives of other South African men and women – whose stories have so much to teach us, and which have, until recently, been ignored though not forgotten.

2
NTSIKANA

Vuyani Booi

Ntsikana, the Xhosa prophet, formed an important link between the traditional and the modern worlds. His story is the story of the penetration of Christianity into the eastern regions of the Cape colony. It is the story of faithful, earnest and zealous missionary enterprise. But it is also the story of a clash of cultures: the old culture of the Xhosa in juxtaposition with the new European culture of the whites and missionaries. Ntsikana was the first Xhosa-speaker to convert to Christianity, to preach the Gospel of Christ, and to compose hymns. He laid the ground for the future translation of the Scriptures into the vernacular.

NTSIKANA'S CHILDHOOD AND YOUTH

Ntsikana came from the Cirha clan – a royal clan closely linked to the Rharhabe chiefdom of the western Xhosa, who lived in the area around the Keiskamma River. His father was a councillor to the Rharhabe king, Ngqika, and a polygamist with two wives. 'Nonabe, the mother of Ntsikana, was the Right Hand (junior) wife. Ntsikana was brought up among his mother's kinsmen until he was about five or six years old. His father then sent for him, having secured his rights by paying a beast for the boy's maintenance since infancy. Gaba's Great Wife, Noyiki, tradition holds, had only one child, a daughter, and so she adopted Ntsikana according to custom as Gaba's heir'. From this time, Ntsikana was to make his home in the Great Place of Ngqika in the Thyume Valley on the banks of the Thyume River.

1800 was a transformative year in the young life of Ntsikana. It plunged him into two contradictory worlds. He underwent the cus-

An artist's impression of Ntsikana (c 1780–1821), the Christian prophet, royal counsellor, and hymn-writer. Ntsikana came from the most ancient of all Xhosa royal lineages, the Cirha, and was aligned with the Xhosa King Ngqika throughout his life. It was at Ngqika's Great Place in the Thyume valley that he first heard the message of the missionary Van der Kemp. When he accepted his prophetic role he symbolically washed himself of the red clay worn by traditional Xhosa, thereby signalling a complex relationship with the forces of change on the frontier. While he accepted the spiritual message of Christianity he remained deeply suspicious of the impact of colonists, and seems to have forseen the divisive impact, on the Xhosa, of King Ngqika's collaboration with colonial authorities. Ntsikana was at Ngqika's Great Place when Ngqika's army was defeated by his rival Ndlambe at the great battle of Malinde (or Amalinde) on the Debe Plain in 1818.

tomary circumcision, and was also initiated into the world of Christianity. The first missionary among the Xhosa, Dr Van der Kemp, who had arrived in the Cape in September 1799, had settled among King Ngqika's people. Since Van der Kemp had come sneakingly, as if by accident, the locals named him Nyengana and so he is known throughout history to this day.

Though his stay among the Ngqika was brief, leaving as he did at the end of 1800, Van der Kemp had a formative influence on the young Ntsikana and the Ngqikas. They still talk of the fiery soldier of Christ – Dr Van der Kemp – extolling the heathen Ngqikas to obey the command given by his Master and Saviour – 'Go ye and teach all nations.'

THE BIRTH OF A PROPHET

As he grew older, Ntsikana complained that there was this 'thing' – as he called it – that he could not shake off, which appeared to follow him wherever he went, haunting his very existence. One of Ntsikana's 'hauntings' occurred while he was inspecting his kraal. While admiring his favourite ox, Hulushe, Ntsikana thought he detected something brighter than usual striking the side of his beast. 'As he looked at the animal, [his] face betrayed exciting feelings, and he thus enquired from the lad standing near by: "Do you observe the thing I now see?" The lad, turning his eyes in the direction indicated, replied: "No, I see nothing there." Ntsikana, recovering from his trance, lifted himself from the ground, on which he had meantime stretched himself, and said to the puzzled boy: "You are right; the sight was not meant to be seen by your eyes".'

Another epiphany struck at a wedding ceremony. As was customary at such occasions, the men performed *umdudo* (the wedding dance). Though a keen and capable dancer from adolescence, on this occasion, and to the disappointment of the gathering, Ntsikana is said to have been reluctant to participate in the ritual. After repeated prodding by the crowd, he ultimately conceded and gave a fantastic performance. But something completely unexpected suddenly happened – a gale force wind began to blow, accompanied by lightning and the clapping of thunder. This shocked the crowd and brought Ntsikana to a sudden halt. Ntikana started dancing again when the phenomenon disappeared. But that was not the end of it, as the narrative goes:

> Immediately the gale arises once more! Again Ntsikana returns to his seat, crest-fallen as ever; and the wind ceases. A third time, he gets up, and a third time this horrid gale arises as furiously as ever. The interested and superstitious gazers exchange looks of astonishment at this strange occurrence repeating itself each time the son of Gaba rises to join the dance! Who has bewitched him?

This experience prompted Ntsikana to leave the wedding ceremony early, much to the astonishment of his two wives.

The Xhosa novelist and educator AC Jordan described the light that appeared in the earlier incident around his kraal as an 'illumination of the soul…' According to Jordan, Ntsikana realised that his life task was to spread the word of God. But it took the later incident at the dance to convince Ntsikana that the 'thing' that had been haunting him was actually a calling to Christianity, to become an agent of the Gospel. The wind represented the power of the supernatural forces, combined with the missionary doctrine, that pulled Ntsikana out of his own culture and religion.

It was a 'slow evolution' that made Ntsikana a stranger among his own people. But though the evolution was slow, the gale wind became a turning point in the life of Ntsikana. It was after this incident that Ntsikana threw 'aside his blanket, plunged himself into the water and washed off all the red ochre that painted his body'. The throwing aside of his blanket could be analyzed as an effort to disown and discard his culture and traditions, while the water was a symbolic representation of Christian baptism: washing off all the red ochre that painted his body was a symbolised washing away of sins committed.

Now a Christian, Ntsikana renounced polygamy. He divorced one of his two wives, Nomonto. At this time it would seem as if he was ready to begin his ministry among his people. But he had competition.

Vying for the ear of his people was Nxele, a one-time witch doctor, now akin to a clairvoyant. What was most disturbing was that many chiefs were listening to him. Feel Ntsikana's exasperation:

'uNxele ubuquqekile, ubalahlekisela nina abantu?' (Nxele has turned upside down, why does he mislead the people?)

A CONFLICTED MISSIONARY AGENT

Though committing himself to Christianity, Ntsikana nonetheless still experienced a conflict between indigenous belief systems (*Inkolo yakwaNtu*) and the foreign belief system (*Inkolo yaseMzini*). He was not ignorant of the fact that the civilisation and religion of white men demanded the sacrifice of other cultures and belief systems, while it positioned itself as 'the' culture and belief system from which civilisation of other nations had to proceed.

But the symbolic washing away of red ochre was akin to washing away a substance which had ingrained itself into the practitioner's skin and blood and become part of the believer's system. Red ochre represents Xhosa culture, traditions and indigenous belief systems. It was in fact impossible to wash these away. Ntsikana was to incorporate these into the hybrid creed that he disseminated among his own people.

His was an ongoing tension. Earlier, whilst still a boy, he had refused to be baptised by white missionaries, even though he claimed to have accepted Christianity. This conflict was not unusual among Xhosa converts, and merging the Christian Gospel with traditional belief systems was a major challenge that all missionaries of the time had to deal with.

Ntsikana conceptualised and constructed his religion in a way that would attract and accommodate the various cultural dimensions of his own people. Because of that fusion, Ntsikana was able to advance Christian beliefs within the African community. He established various congregations in the Transkei: Fort Beaufort, Mankazana Valley, Somerset East, Burnshill, Debe Nek, King William's Town and at Mgwali. Among his initial recruits were King Ngqika, Noyi and Matshikwe

Many people visit Ntsikana's grave at eThwathwa, near Fort Beaufort.

(Ntsikana's two closest friends), Kobe and Dukwana (his sons), Soga (Ngqika's counsellor) and Zaze and Festiri Soga (Soga's sons), and the Jwara clan of Soga.

Ntsikana acknowledges his Christian influence over the Soga household, which was later to produce the towering figure of Reverend Tiyo Soga, in one of his hymns: *'Lomzi kaKhonwana siwubizile'* (The house of Khonwana has been called). Khonwana was a nickname for 'Old' Soga. Winning over Soga, a councillor to King Ngqika, was particularly astute of Ntsikana. Old Soga influenced the king and thus enabled others within the community to follow their king into Christianity.

NTSIKANA, MUSICIAN AND COMPOSER

Ntsikana's success also owed much to his musical compositions. To him, singing was just as important as preaching. He composed several hymns that spoke to the cultural and traditional experiences of Africans. They appealed to the (lyrical) nature of Africans and the hymns are now regarded as classics and still sung today.

'UMDALI WOBOMI' ('LIFE CREATOR')

He! Nanku'mdali bom wase sikolweni
He! Nanku'mdali bom osibize sihleli
He! Nanku'mdali bom wasinga phezulu

(See! There stands the Life Creator; he of the school
See! There stands the Life Creator; who calls us to rise
See! There stands the Life Creator; he has ascended)

'INGOMA ENGQUKUVA' ('THE ROUND HYMN')

Elele hom-na Elele hom-na
Latsho e-Gqora; Hom-na Cibini le
Latsho kwaGaga; Hom, hom-na nakwaMankazana
Lafika lathetha; Hom; hom-na! Elele, le

(It was proclaimed at Gqora: Hom hom-na
Also at the Lake of Arms (Peddie): Hom hom-na
It was proclaimed at Gaga: Hom, hom-na
Likewise at Mankazana: Hom, hom-na
There it arrived to speak: Hom, hom-na
Halleluja. Amen: Hom, hom-na).

'ULO THIXO OMKHULU' ('HE IS THE GREAT GOD')

(*This song was further arranged by John Knox Bokwe.*)
He, is the Great God, who is heaven
Thou art thou, shield of truth
Thou art thou, stronghold of truth
Thou art thou, thicket of truth
Thou art thou who dwellest in the highest …

AN ORGANIC INTELLECTUAL

The very first intellectual among the Southern Nguni, Ntsikana inspired a whole new generation of African scholars. These included his son, William Kobe Ntsikana, who was one of Lovedale's first pupils and became a writer, Zaze Soga, and Makhaphela Noyi Balfour (a friend of Kobe's and a prominent writer). Most importantly, though, Ntsikana was a pioneer of African hymn-writing – something that had been unheard of before. His compositions were inspired by his cultural background and drew from African experiences and idioms.

King Ngqika recognised Ntsikana's intellect and drew him closer to serve as a royal advisor. Legend has it that Ntsikana made several prophecies that actually materialised.

One was about the battle of Malinde in 1818 against the rival chief Ndlambe, Ngqika's uncle, who questioned Ngqika's policy towards the British colonists and the leadership status the colonists conferred on him. He had gathered great support among the Xhosa. Ntsikana's

It is said that Ntsikana used this stone as a bell to summon his followers for religious gatherings and imbizos. *It is still to be found on the slopes of a small stony hill at Ngqika's Great Place in the Thyume Valley.*

prophecy apparently went as follows: 'go and call Ngqika; tell him some calamity, I do not know what, is about to happen. I see the heads of the Ngqikas being devoured by ants.' This prophecy of Ntsikana echoed what Nxele of Balala announced: that Ngqika's people 'were going to become firewood and ants'. Ntsikana had earlier dismissed Nxele's prophecy as misleading the people. Now, the battle annihilated the Ngqika supporters and claimed the lives of many Ngqika warriors. Ntsikana apparently protested bitterly against this war and 'with prophetic foresight, warned, and implored the King, Chiefs and Councilors and people, to let it alone … Ngqika paid no regard, and their heads were devoured by ants.'

Another prophecy was about the impending arrival of the Mfengu among Xhosas.

> … a time is coming when you will see people whom you have never seen before, whose ears, which are bored, are like the curve of a dried ox-skin. Be careful of those people; do not receive them to dwell among you, but let them pass unmolested. If you receive them, they will raise their 'stuff' and leave it on you, if you do not heed these words. I see this country white with wagon roads. I see flocks of sheep grazing on it. I see this land studded with white houses. There are those present who will bear me witness; but beware of strange doctrine, it will mislead many.

By 1820, Ntsikana's health started failing him and he eventually passed on the following year at his kraal at Thwatwa. His hymns lived on and continue to be popular to this day. His adaptation of Christianity to African beliefs was to inspire what later came to be known as black theology.

A young Tiyo Soga. Tiyo Soga (1829–1871) was the first black South African to be educated overseas (in Glasgow) and the first black South African priest to be ordained overseas. Well known as a newspaper writer, he also translated many English works of literature into Xhosa, and composed several hymns. Although a Christian missionary, he was outspoken against the racism that was so much a part of the colonial mission. Soga was a defender of 'native' viewpoints and values, and as such was a grandfather of black theology and black consciousness. He was the subject of the first biography of a black South African, written in 1877 by JA Chalmers.

3
TIYO SOGA

Mcebisi Ndletyana

The first internationally educated black South African and priest, a pioneer of African literature, and a seminal intellectual, Tiyo Soga embodied the paradox of the civilising mission. He personified the modernising influence of the missionary enterprise, but was also an indictment of the supposed moral virtue of the colonial establishment. Towards the end of his brief, but illustrious, life (he died aged 42), Soga turned his educational training towards awakening the very same national pride and consciousness that his missionary teachers had denounced. Soga's ideas were the precursor of nationalist thought, and sowed the seeds of black consciousness and black theology in South Africa.

FAMILY AND EARLY YEARS

Soga was born in 1829 at Mgwali on the eastern frontier of the Cape colony. His mother, Nosutu, was one of eight wives and bore nine children. Tiyo was the seventh born and had 29 siblings – his father's polygamy being an indication of his relative wealth and social standing in the community. Known as 'Old Soga', his father was an advisor to King Ngqika and a veteran of many frontier wars against colonial conquest. Naming his son after one of the royal councillors – also a distinguished soldier – Old Soga hoped that Tiyo would follow a similar path.

Tiyo certainly experienced the turbulence of colonial conquest first hand throughout his life. He was born in the year that his people were expelled from their ancestral land – an event his illiterate mother later remembered as marking the year of Tiyo's birth. Missionary patronage, however, steered the young Tiyo towards new ground. While still at elementary school, he was brought under the wing of a Scottish Presbyterian missionary, Reverend William Chalmers. The missionary had discerned great potential in the young lad and thought a suitable environment would unleash it. Christian converts themselves (although in truth Old Soga was only a nominal Christian)' Tiyo's parents were more than happy to have their son receive missionary tutelage. They were among the early recruits of the first-ever African missionary, Ntsikana, and lived by Christian values. In keeping with these values, Tiyo was never circumcised. No matter his personal religious beliefs, Old Soga appreciated the benefits of modern influence. In 1835 he became a pioneer of modern farming techniques among his community. Tiyo was not the only member of his family to receive a missionary education – one of his brothers, Festiri, became a teacher.

EDUCATION

Under the auspices of Reverend Chalmers, Soga proved an ardent and devout pupil. This determined not only his future career choice, but also his prospects of academic advancement. Reverend Chalmers got him admitted into the prestigious Lovedale Seminary in 1844 and paid his exorbitant tuition fee. This was despite the fact that Tiyo had failed an earlier admission test. Reverend Chalmers was taken by Tiyo's responsiveness to his teachings and believed that his failure didn't reflect a poor intellect, but ill-preparation due to a poor educational background. Time at a good school, concluded Chalmers, would bring out Tiyo's true potential. Thus, at the age of fifteen, Tiyo began a course of intense academic instruction for the first time in his life.

But the turmoil of colonial conflict intervened in Soga's life again at this time. Lovedale Seminary closed (temporarily) two years after Tiyo arrived there due to yet another frontier war. Suspected of colluding with the colonial authorities, Reverend Chalmers and other Presbyterian missionaries fled back to Glasgow, in Scotland. They took Soga with them out of fear that, as a Christian convert, his native community would ostracise him. The missionaries resolved that he should

Lovedale Seminary College, which was started in 1824. The missionary Reverend William Chalmers paid for Soga to attend the prestigious Lovedale Seminary College in Alice from 1844 until 1846, when the College closed temporarily, due to war on the frontier. Prior to this, Soga had come under missionary influence at his parents' home in Mgwali. Soga left Lovedale with the missionaries, to go to the city of Glasgow, in Scotland, for the first of two formative visits. He returned to take up the job of headmaster of Uniondale mission school in Keiskammahoek in 1849.

further his theological studies abroad. Thus, in July 1846, Soga began a life-long relationship with the city of Glasgow, a place he would come to call 'home'.

TRAVEL ABROAD

The architecture of Glasgow, compared to that of his native village, awed the young lad. Soga hadn't thought it possible that people were capable of such ingenuity. However, Glasgow also relieved Soga of his naivety about the moral compass of the Western world. An incident involving the theft of his books and a satchel, which he had trustfully left just outside the door of a house facing the street, shattered his illusion that all Scots were morally upright.

In Glasgow, Soga affirmed his faith through baptism, and embarked on serious theological training at the Free Church Seminary School. By the time he graduated two years later as a catechist, Soga couldn't wait to return home as a missionary.

MISSIONARY WORK

Back in the Cape colony by January 1849, Soga plunged into missionary work. He quickly rose to the position of schoolmaster at Uniondale missionary school at Keiskamma Hoek, the next year.

But the war of 1850 forced Soga to a crossroads: he had to make a choice between continuing on the missionary path, and joining the anti-colonial resistance. Thus far he'd never had to make that choice. Until now, at every confrontation, his parents or the missionaries had chosen on his behalf. This time, his chief, Maqoma, personally called on him to choose which side he was on. Hoping to obtain intelligence about the military tactics of the enemy, Maqoma asked Soga to translate letters they had confiscated from British soldiers. Soga declined the request, stating that he 'would not mix himself up in a context which carried death to his fellow creatures'. That decision placed him squarely behind the missionary enterprise. In Maqoma's eyes, he became an accomplice in the colonial project, deserving a similar fate to that of his missionary brethren.

SCOTLAND AGAIN

Thus, once again, in June 1851, Soga departed with fellow missionaries for the refuge of Scotland. However, this visit imprinted his name on the annals of missionary records. Soga became the first African student ever to enroll at Glasgow University's Theological Hall. But his poor schooling hadn't prepared him for the rigour of tertiary education, and he found the curriculum quite daunting. Without the precedent of higher education in his family or community, and far away in a foreign land, Soga never quite mustered the self-confidence to distinguish himself academically. (He later admitted as much to his children and encouraged them to be self-confident.)

Social life in Scotland didn't provide much solace either. Soga was looked upon as an exotic figure, against which the Scottish public tested its racial prejudice. The depth of his character, however, stood him in good stead. In Soga, none of the racial prejudice about his kind was ever confirmed and, as one of his university professors said later, his friends would even 'forget that he was a kaffir, but could not well forget that he was a gentleman'.

Others, however, couldn't see beyond his complexion, but simply saw an object of amusement and study. Soga received dinner invitations, only to be asked to provide entertainment by talking in his foreign language and singing native hymns. He soon learnt to decline social invitations, limiting social activity to a minimum. This bred loneliness and misery. On 20 December 1854, he scribbled in his diary:

> What assures me that I shall see next year? I hope I shall. Well, but hope is not certainty; and though it often realises its object, it is as often disappointed. My life hangs by the feeblest and most attenuated thread, which the gentlest breath may sever. The insignificant fly may alight upon it and break it.

Soga persevered, however. He graduated on 22 September 1856, and was ordained the next day, through sheer determination. He had dug deep inside himself for inspiration, and would often do this later when confronted by racially inspired colonial scepticism.

He never developed blind resentment against white people, however, and he married a Scottish woman, Janet Burnside, on 27 February 1857. An invitation to the wedding reveals the sense of humour that endeared him to his classmates.

> Come and witness the final execution of the sentence against the criminal, and give me the benefit of your mutual benefit before I shall be launched into the horrors of matrimony. Ker, of Campbell Street, will be the executioner. The terrible tragedy takes place in Iboxholm, Paisley Road, at twelve o'clock noon.

The mission station at Mgwali, Eastern Cape. Soga returned here as an ordained priest in 1857 at the end of his second, eight-year-long trip to Scotland. He revived the mission station, which included a school and hostel for girls. In 1957 Soga also became the first black South African ever to preach (in Port Elizabeth) at a white church. Soga resolved then to use 'boldness of speech', and by the early 1860s he was becoming increasingly outspoken against white prejudice in his newspaper writing.

The first ordained African priest, and married to a white woman to boot, Soga returned to South Africa on 2 July 1857 and became the most prominent African of his time. He was second only to the West African pioneer, Edward Wilmot Blyden. He quickly grew into a staunch defender of the much-maligned African masses, an exponent of their racial identity, and a fervent agent of Christianity and civilisation among the natives.

A PROMINENT AFRICAN

But Soga began his public career cautiously, held back by a concern not to say anything that would turn official opinion against missionary activity. Relations between the missionaries and colonial society were delicate, as the former often counselled against colonial aggression and prejudice toward the natives. Soga was himself ambivalent about the predisposition of settlers towards natives. On the one hand, the positive welcome he received upon his arrival made him believe that colonial race-relations would soon change for the better:

> Times are changed ... Although there are among certain classes here, strong prejudices against colour, yet my reception showed that these prejudices are not so much against the skin as against the circumstances and the character of those whose complexion I bear.

On the other hand, Soga remained acutely aware that prejudice was engrained within colonial culture. The settler community, he believed, simply tolerated him because of his education and missionary standing: 'the Scotch education, not my black face, has been my passport into places where that face would not be permitted to enter'. Thus Soga resolved 'never to force myself into their company ... Knowing the prejudice existing in the colony against colour, I had resolved never to break forcibly through these prejudices.'

Indeed, colonial prejudice wouldn't allow Soga to forget that, though accomplished, he was, after all, still a native. One of many indignities he would suffer in later life included being stopped by policemen who demanded that he produce a pass. It was not enough that Soga told them that he was exempted from carrying one, due to his 'civilised status'. The policemen led him off to prison where they proceeded to interrogate him on why he, a native, did not carry a pass.

STANDING AGAINST RACISM

Unrelenting colonial aggression brought him out of his cautionary approach to racial issues. By the early 1860s, Soga had taken a firm public stance against racism and colonial expansion. On one occasion, in June 1864, he lambasted the colonial media as a mouthpiece of commercial interests. It feigned pretexts for war, Soga explained, in order to confiscate more native land. He concluded with a subtle caricature of such war-mongers as charlatans who hid behind the cloak of civilisation, being, in fact, less civilised themselves: 'Warriors of noble spirit disdain to strike a foe without weapons ... it is beneath the dignity of civilised men to be the formidable enemy of naked barbarians, who cannot write and reason like themselves'.

Pervasive though it was, Soga never allowed racial prejudice to alter his self-perception. Where the bigoted colonists expected him to falter, he thrived. Soga revelled in disproving racial scepticism. When he

Soga's Scottish wife, Janet Soga, in South Africa. They married on 27 February, 1857. During his time in Scotland Soga had felt socially isolated much of the time, but had not allowed this to develop into prejudice against whites. Janet Soga returned to South Africa with him and outlived him. They had seven children.

became the first African priest ever to receive an invitation to preach at a white church, in Port Elizabeth in July 1857, Soga wrote about the expectations of his audience, and his response:

> I have no doubt that some came with the object of hearing and then laughing at the ridiculous blunders and nonsense of a Kafir preacher. Such thoughts often passed my mind, and became motives to courage and boldness of speech. There are times when the very means which malice and prejudice make use of to ensnare, annoy, or put down a man, become sources of strength.

The sermon received a glowing review in the local newspaper, the *Port Elizabeth Telegraph*, on 9 July 1857: 'In this person may be seen the transcendent operation and effects of Christianity, civilisation, and science trampling under foot every opposing prejudice and difficulty, however formidable or seemingly insurmountable'.

Such flattering reviews echoed Soga's own beliefs about civilisation and race-relations. If it did not achieve total reprieve from racism, the educational elevation of natives would at least change colonial perceptions towards natives. Once educated, natives would rise up beyond their servitude to colonial society. Thus, Soga considered himself singularly responsible for leading his fellow natives into civilisation.

He extended missionary influence further into native territories, in the face of pessimism and lack of financial support from the Glasgow Missionary Society.

In his first posting at Mgwali in 1857, Soga revived the mission station, which had been abandoned during the last frontier war. Four years later, as his congregation expanded, Soga built the first modern church ever built within a native territory by a Presbyterian missionary. The Mission Society wasn't keen on such a construction. They thought the natives too indifferent towards Christianity to warrant an expense of that magnitude and feared that they would burn it in the event of another war breaking out. Soga was therefore left to raise more than two-thirds of the £1 464 it cost to build the church. Two more churches followed, in Tutuka and Quoloka.

A NEW WORLD VIEW

To be truly successful, however, Soga contended that missionaries had to completely redefine their philosophical approach when working among the natives. Put in modern terms, Christianity had to be foregrounded within Afrocentrism. This would require a profound philosophical shift within the missionary enterprise. Missionaries had always denounced the values of natives as barbaric and thus not worth learning about. Theirs was a paternalistic approach based on an assumption that they already knew everything they needed to know. But Soga railed against such paternalism and counselled: 'the knot of the Kafir's prejudices and habits is not to be rudely cut, by the uncompromising knife of civilised tastes. It must be patiently and cautiously untied'. According to Soga, missionaries had to work from within the native world-view, outwardly. The natives, he advised, '… prefer to be drawn, rather than driven'. This demanded that missionaries 'be prepared to identify themselves with the people' and, in the process, they would actually discover that natives are not without virtue:

> the student of human nature can reap a splendid harvest in the study of their history, prejudices, habits, and customs … he will find much to show that there is some good in all … that God is the common Father of all, and therefore that no race should be despised.

Soga turned the civilising project on its back. He interrogated the cultural assumptions that underpinned it. Rather than simply accepting the virtues of whiteness, on the one hand, and acceding to the supposed vices of blackness, on the other, Soga held them both up to the same level of scrutiny. He asserted that such criminal practices as cattle-theft among natives were just as morally deplorable as 'the refined thieving of forgery, embezzlement, and voluntary insolvency' common among white criminals. Modernity, Soga believed, was not a function of race, but socialisation. He explained this in a letter: 'The Inheritance of my Children', he wrote for his sons around 1870 upon realising that he didn't have long to live: 'It is only circumstances, in the providence of God, that have made a difference of natural capacity and intelligence.

Under favourable circumstances the reason of the black man is capable of as much improvement and enlightenment as that of the white'.

Thus Soga would often discard notions that he was an exception among natives, asserting that he 'knew of many who would have far excelled him …' He wouldn't let stereotypes pass unchallenged, to a point where his missionary colleagues thought him 'overly-sensitive', something they considered a character flaw. It made them uncomfortable, since they had to be overly-cautious of what they said in his company, lest their prejudice showed.

LITERARY CULTURE AND NATIVE UPLIFTMENT

Soga viewed literary culture as key to native upliftment. This drew him into the literary world. From 1860, Soga translated English works into Xhosa, and thus widened readership among Xhosas. These works included articles that appeared in missionary journals, John Bunyan's *Pilgrim's Progress* (published in 1866, though he had started the translation at university), and the Bible (which he didn't live to see published).

Soga's passion for African literature partly stemmed from his self-perception as a public intellectual. He believed that 'Missionaries must show that they can speak on other questions than those in which they are more immediately interested'. He took to developing African literature with even greater urgency as his health deteriorated in the mid-1860s. His health had begun to suffer seriously back in the 1850s (and was eventually diagnosed as chronic laryngitis in 1866). Fearing that he didn't have long to live, in March 1865 Soga requested the Mission Society to grant him retirement from active missionary work so that he could '… endeavour to lay the foundation for a native literature of which our people are in great need'. But his request was declined because the Society considered Soga to be the most able and dedicated missionary doing evangelical work among natives.

Newspaper writing also occupied much of Soga's engagement as a public intellectual. He was an indefatigable contributor. Because natives were 'conversational people and always eager for news,' Soga wrote in the debut edition of *Indaba* (August 1862), that 'newspapers would appeal to their nature. Natives would look eagerly to receiving the next edition of the paper, just as they would look forward to receiving a stranger in order to hear news from other parts of the country'.

Soga's literary influence was also felt in lyrical compositions – he compiled a book of hymns in 1860. This aspect of his work had actually begun in 1850, when he composed his first hymns.

SOGA'S LEGACY

In many ways, Soga was the first nationalist-intellectual and a progenitor of black consciousness – an ideology that would be popularised a century later by Steve Biko. Soga placed a great premium not only on preserving the history of South Africa, but also on his, and future generations', knowing that history. When not engaged in missionary work, Soga interviewed elders on history, fables, legends, customs and the genealogy of chiefs, and wrote articles which he published in newspapers. He urged unity among all black people beyond the ethnic divide: '… to a weak party or race, union, above all things, is strength'. Because they are 'degraded, despised, down-trodden people' his 'advice to all coloured people' was: 'assist one another; patronise talent in one another; prefer one another's business, shops, &c., just for the reason that it is better to prefer and elevate kindred and countrymen before all others'. This was the only way, Soga reasoned, blacks 'would raise their influence and positions among their white neighbours'. Proud black man that he was, Soga advised his children that, though born to a white mother, they should identify themselves as black men in order to gain respect in life:

> if you wish to gain credit for yourselves – if you do not wish to feel the taunt of men, which you sometimes may be made to feel – take your place in the world as coloured, not as white men; as Kafirs not as Englishmen. You will be more thought of for this by all good and wise

people, than for the other. It will show them that you care not for the slight put by the prejudices of men upon one class of men, who happen to differ from them in complexion.

Ultimately, Soga was a cultural hybrid. He extolled British culture because of the benefits afforded it by enlightenment and he regarded himself as a willing subject of Queen Victoria – whom he looked up to as 'the best friend of all men'. Soga wished to reproduce that enlightenment in South Africa, but he didn't reject African cultural influence. He still observed some African norms, such as submitting to the authority of native royalty. Soga thought highly of chiefs, describing them as 'specimens of Nature's own nobility'. And, unlike the rest of his missionary brethren, he considered them reasonable: 'If you speak sense, these men are sure to understand thoroughly, although they may not receive your message.'

The church at Mgwali which was built by Soga and is still used today. In addition to being a prominent writer of opinion pieces in newspapers, Soga was a dedicated missionary and raised money to build the new church at Mgwali. Two more churches followed, in Tutuka (where he died) and Quoloka, in the Eastern Cape.

At the end, it was his dedication to missionary work that accelerated, if not, ended Soga's life. After ten years in Mgwali, he was transferred to Tutuka (in what later became Transkei) to initiate missionary work. The climate was damp and humid, and disagreeable to Soga's health. He died at 2:45 on Saturday afternoon, 12 August 1871, leaving behind his wife and seven children. His four oldest sons William Anderson, John Henderson, Kirkland Allan and Jotello Festiri later distinguished themselves in public life in the fields of journalism, literature, medicine and law. Soga had sent his three oldest sons to Scotland in 1870, when his health deteriorated, in order to escape racism in South Africa, and to receive tertiary education. But he also urged them to return and 'live for the elevation of your degraded, despised, downtrodden people'.

4

JOHN TENGO JABAVU

Mcebisi Ndletyana

A pioneer of African journalism and champion of higher education for Africans, yet woefully dependant on white-liberal agency, John Tengo Jabavu was ultimately a conflicted figure.

Jabavu was one of six children. He was born in January 1859 at the village of Tyotyora, about seven kilometres from Fort Beaufort. The mission school of Healdtown had been established here, and both his parents were regular church-goers. His father, Ntwanambi, was a precentor and a prayer-leader – like their father, both John and one of his brothers would later lead singing and prayers in church. He worked as a seasonal labourer building roads and doing masonry work in Grahamstown. Jabavu's mother, Mary, worked as a washer-woman and sold tin dishes.

EARLY LIFE AND MARRIAGE

Though both his parents were illiterate, Jabavu went on to achieve academic honours. Starting elementary school at the age of ten, he excelled in Literature and Mathematics and repeatedly won the quarterly academic competitions at school. In 1875 he received a Teachers' Certificate, after his father paid for the exam by selling one of his valued ploughing oxen, 'Falteyn'. This achievement was followed by yet another distinction, in 1883, when Jabavu passed matric. He became one of only three people within the black community at that time with a matric, the others being Percy Frames and Simon Sihlali.

In 1885 Jabavu married Elda Sakuba, also a Healdtown girl. She was the daughter of Reverend James B Sakuba (1833–1893), who was

John Tengo Jabavu (1859–1921). Jabavu was a prominent black thinker and educator, writer, friend of white liberals, and supporter of the Afrikaner Bond. His passion for journalism led him to become a prominent newspaper man and former of black opinion. Although his political views were at odds with those of most other black leaders, often seeming to fly in the face of black interests, he made a lasting contribution to university education for black men and women in South Africa, helping to establish Fort Hare University.

Healdtown mission school. Jabavu was born in at the village of Tyotyora, where Healdtown mission school had been established after the colonial government decided to give financial support to institutions that would train school teachers and evangelists. Jabavu embodied the ideological conflicts facing mission-educated Xhosa men and women in the Eastern Cape at the time. He received an education at Healdtown and first started work as a teacher, before going on to work at the missionary newspaper Isigidimi Sama-Xosa. Jabavu undoubtedly eclipsed colonial expectations of educated natives when he started his own newspaper.

one of the earliest black Wesleyan priests. Elda was chosen by Jabavu's mother, who had disapproved of his own choice for marriage. The marriage bore four sons, but Elda's life came to an untimely end in 1900. Quickly thereafter, Jabavu married Getrude Joninga, with whom he had three daughters.

JOURNALIST AND OPINION-MAKER

Jabavu began his professional teaching career as a teenager, aged seventeen. His first job was in Somerset East. Journalism, however, proved to be a much stronger calling for the young Jabavu. While still teaching in Somerset East, he apprenticed at the local newspaper, learning about the technical side of the newspaper business. This entailed a gruelling schedule for the aspiring journalist. He would start his apprentice work in the early hours of the morning, work till breakfast, then go to his teaching job. In the midst of all this – and while taking part-time studies in Greek and Latin – Jabavu also began writing for publication. This was the start of what would become a life-long involvement with newspapers. He became a regular contributor to the *Cape Argus,* becoming friends with the then editor, Mr Saul Solomon.

Now a writer of note and a somewhat knowledgeable press man, Jabavu left teaching after six years in 1881 to take over the editorship of *Isigidimi Sama-Xosa (Xhosa Express)* at Lovedale. His stay there was brief, and he left at the expiry of his three-year contract in 1883. The largely religious focus of the missionary-owned newspaper was too restrictive for someone with his strong interest in political issues. However, while at *Isigidimi,* he had devoted a significant number of pages of the paper to parliamentary debates. He granted positive coverage to liberal politicians – Saul Solomon, JX Merriman, JW Sauer, and RW Rose-Innes – who supported the franchise for Africans, and seemed to show an interest in the general welfare of Africans.

Staff huts at Healdtown mission school.

Jabavu's departure from *Isigidimi* turned out to be a blessing for civic education among African voters in the Cape and for black journalism in general. A political 'junkie', Jabavu became a political agent and canvasser for Rose-Innes in the 1884 elections for the Victoria East seat. Rose-Innes won, largely thanks to Jabavu's involvement, for which he had refused remuneration. Following the advice of his friend, Meshack Pelem, Jabavu founded the very first black secular newspaper. Its objective was to inform the African population about public issues, and promote their participation in the electoral process. Named *Imvo Zabantsundu (Native Opinion)*, and founded with the financial support of Messrs James Weir and RW Rose-Innes, the newspaper went to print in November 1884, with John Tengo Jabavu as its editor. He was only 24 years old then.

Imvo was to become the voice of liberal politics in the Cape and an advocate of African interests. Often, Jabavu's interests and those of his liberal financiers coincided and the black public was the better for it. Ultimately, though, *Imvo* privileged the interests of its financiers, and they were not always the same as the Africans'. However, for a while, *Imvo* vociferously championed the interests of the black populace. Editorials informed them about parliamentary matters and the performance of their elected representatives, and discussed the advantages of voting for one candidate over another. *Imvo* also put up a vocal opposition to pass laws and unrestrained sale of alcohol to the black population.

But, where the interests of the financiers of *Imvo* and its black readership conflicted, Jabavu chose to support the former. This happened frequently, from the late 1880s onwards, over several key issues: franchise qualification for Africans; support for the Anglo-Boer War; political unity among blacks against the colonial establishment; and the Land Act of 1913. On the franchise, for instance, the liberal politicians that Jabavu had helped to office, also known as 'Friends of the Natives', now supported restrictions on the black franchise, and hoped to limit the number of eligible black voters. Jabavu continued to support them, despite this conflict of interests.

Jabavu's newspaper, Imvo Zabantsundu *(Native Opinion), was started in 1884. It had the financial support of the white liberal politicians. In this way, he was closely linked with white capitalist interests, and his editorials on issues such as the native franchise and land ownership became increasingly out of tune with opinions voiced by other prominent black leaders. However, he was an independent thinker, and alienated those same liberals when he backed Afrikaner Bond politicians in the lead-up to the Anglo-Boer War. His political image was tarnished by his support for the infamous Land Act of 1913, which every other black leader decried. Sol Plaatje was one of the leaders who disagreed with Jabavu over the political direction he was advocating.*

Jabavu's implicit support for the white politicians, who were the nemesis of African voters, turned vocal in the 1898 elections. He supported and formed an electoral pact with the Afrikaner Bond. This was a party that had made it its life-long mission to eliminate voting rights for Africans. Bond politicians had felt disadvantaged by African voters who consistently and *en masse* voted for the English-speaking liberal politicians. The following year, as the English and the Boers went to war, Jabavu lent his support to the latter. This was a deviation on Jabavu's part, as he had earlier undertaken to focus the newspaper more 'on measures than the men who advocate them'. Yet, in the instance of the war, the measure did not seem to matter and he essentially followed the men – Merriman and Sauer – who had become close associates of the Bond by 1898.

Jabavu's support took the form of flattering editorials on Hofmeyr's leadership qualities, as well as exhortations to South African voters to support the South African Party. It would have made sense for Jabavu to side with the British, in the light of his professed loyalty to the Crown and his status as a beneficiary of the 'civilising mission'. However, Jabavu took a decidedly sympathetic view towards the Boers. He saw the war as an act of British provocation, with the British bent on extending their authority over the Boer republics. (Yet he had always supported British colonialism over Africans, because of what he called the 'civilising' benefits of colonialism).

While puzzling to others, Jabavu considered his stance on the Anglo-Boer War to be part of his journalistic duty to 'speak straight from his heart'. His readership, he reasoned, would respond to his frank views, and would not care to see him acting as '… a charlatan who poses to guide and instruct it with his tongue in his cheek on what he may sometimes not believe in'.

Unsurprisingly, Jabavu earned enormous derision from liberal politicians who had previously supported him, particularly RW Rose-Innes and James W Weir. Rose-Innes denounced Jabavu's views as 'disloyal and seditious and, were martial law in force, this district would

In this early editorial (1884) on white objections to black voters, Jabavu describes the liberal politician, Rose-Innes, whose parliamentary seat he had secured by canvassing for black votes, as 'appearing on the scene as a veritable modern Hercules to lay the demon of negrophobia'.

subject you to immediate arrest and imprisonment'. Both Rose-Innes and Weir publicly announced that they were withdrawing their subscription and support for *Imvo*. Mercury Printing Press, its printers from inception, ended their contract with *Imvo*, forcing it to start using the Watchman Printing Works. And the paper was banned on 19 August 1901 (only to reappear in October 1902) under Martial Law for the King William's Town district promulgated in January 1901.

SPLIT WITH BLACK LEADERSHIP

Jabavu's support for the end of the African franchise alienated him from the broader black leadership. The split within the black middle class culminated in the formation of a rival newspaper, *Izwi Labantu*, in 1897 – an unashamedly African newspaper that lent its support to the emerging African nationalist cause. Its very title, *The Voice of the People*, suggested a more militant predisposition than the moderately titled *Native Opinion*.

The founders of *Izwi*, including Reverend Rubusana, were pivotal in the initiatives that eventually led to the formation of the South African Native National Congress in 1912 (SANNC, later the ANC). Jabavu refused to be part of the SANNC, objecting to its racial exclusivity, and formed his own non-racial organisation instead, the South African Races Congress.

Jabavu's differences with other black leaders resurfaced over the Land Act of 1913. He supported the discriminatory legislation. Every other black leader opposed it, because it sought to limit the proportion of land inhabited by the majority black population to a pitiful 13 per cent of the entire land surface.

His support for the Land Act generated an acrimonious and public exchange between himself and Sol Plaatje, a journalist and founding member of the ANC. In one exchange, Jabavu reported that a meeting of Africans in King William's Town supported the Grobler-Sauer Bill (which eventually became the Land Act). Sol Plaatje disputed this, and later proved the assertion to be false. Plaatje had taken the long trip from Mafikeng to King William's Town with the singular purpose of disproving Jabavu. While in King William's Town, Plaatje also attempted to meet with Jabavu. He made four attempts, and failed in all of them. After providing different excuses for the first three requests, on the fourth attempt Jabavu flatly refused to meet Plaatje. He chose to lock himself in his office instead.

Jabavu downplayed Plaatje's subsequent reports of African opposition towards the Act. The meeting that Plaatje attended, Jabavu explained, only reflected urban opinion. Rural opinion was quite the opposite. Plaatje responded:

> Now, I challenge Imvo, or Mr. Tengo-Jabavu, to call a series of three public meetings, anywhere in the district of King Williamstown. Let us both address these meetings immediately after the Natives Land Act has been read and interpreted to each. We could address the meetings from the same platform, or separately, but on the same day and at the same place. For every vote carried at each of these meetings in favour of his views on the Act I undertake to hand over £15 to the Grey Hospital (King Williamstown), and £15 to the Victoria Hospital (Lovedale), on condition that for every vote I carry at any of these meetings, he hand over £15 to the Victoria Hospital (Mafikeng) and £15 to the Carnavon Hospital (Kimberly). That is £30 for charity, if he will accept. I will not place any difficulties in his way by inviting him to meetings up here, but leave him to call meetings among his own people (if he has any) in his own district, and I will attend at my own expense.

Jabavu declined the challenge. Needless to say, the relationship between the two distinguished journalists soured even further. Plaatje charged that Jabavu could be forgiven for 'fabricating the mess out of imaginary native votes of confidence for his masters' delectation … because his paper is native only in language'. Plaatje went on to imply that Jabavu's 'mind had become the property of someone other than' himself.

Jabavu's rivalry with nationalist leaders also brought a speedy end to black representation in the Cape Provincial Council. In 1914 he challenged Walter Rubusana, the first-ever African to be elected to the

Council in 1909, for his seat. Jabavu's candidature divided the black voters between himself and Rubusana. The latter still got more votes than Jabavu by far – 852 to 294 votes – but fell short of the majority vote. The seat was won by a white candidate instead.

EDUCATIONAL ACTIVIST AND PIONEER

If Jabavu shamed himself politically, he redeemed himself through his legacy in tertiary education. Jabavu had always been passionate about education – a fact evidenced by his activism within the Native Educational Association. This body had periodically published commentary on all native issues, and consistently formed native opinion on these issues. He also conducted an evening school for adults. But now he distinguished himself in African tertiary education by leading a campaign that culminated in the establishment of the very first African University in South Africa in 1916, the University of Fort Hare.

The idea of establishing a university for black students was precipitated by an exodus of black youth to universities in the United States. Black independent churches, through their links with black universities there, were sending more and more students from South Africa to study there. The colonial government was unsettled by this movement. They feared that exposure to the freedom struggle in the United States would radicalise the young South Africans. The colonial government had no desire for them to replicate the freedom struggle once they were back in South Africa.

Jabavu exploited this colonial uneasiness, arguing that the only way to deal with the situation was to establish a local university. The South African Native Affairs Commission agreed, after its hearings on the subject from 1903 to 1905. Jabavu, together with Dr Neil Macvicar and Hobart Houghton (both from Lovedale), travelled countrywide, canvassing support for what was known as the 'Inter-State Native College' scheme. *Imvo* became a mouthpiece for the proposed university. It popularised the idea and urged donations, including a £10 000 donation from the Transkei Territories General Council.

At the opening of Fort Hare, in recognition of his pivotal role in establishing the institution, Jabavu was appointed to the Governing Council. He used this position and influence to shape the profile and the selection policy of the university on two fronts. Firstly, Jabavu insisted that the College also admit women because 'there was no point in educating their young men if their future wives were unable to offer them companionship and community of interest which only an edu-

Jabavu with his second wife, Getrude Joninga, in 1908. The baby is their daughter Dorothy. The boys are three of his four sons by his first wife, Elda Sakuba.

cated woman could give'. Secondly, and to prevent the university becoming elitist, Jabavu persuaded the Council to set its entrance qualification in a way that did not exclude a massive number of applications. He intended it to be as inclusive as possible.

With his dream of a black university realised, Jabavu, who was experiencing ailing health, gradually bowed out of public life. He left the editorship of *Imvo* largely to his son, Alexander. By this time, the newspaper had lost any credibility as the mouthpiece of African interests. This stemmed largely from Jabavu's controversial support of the Land Act.

His central role in founding Fort Hare, however, rehabilitated his image within the African community. Jabavu died in 1921, and Fort Hare came to be known as 'Jabavu's college', cementing Jabavu's legacy in the sphere of education. Two of Jabavu's sons, Davidson Don Tengo and Alexander Macaulay, later emulated their father's achievements in education and public life. Davidson Don Tengo, a Bachelor of Arts graduate from the University of London, was appointed as a lecturer at the newly established Fort Hare and went on to become Professor of Bantu Languages. Outside of the university, he held several leading positions in various political organisations including the Cape Native Voters, the All African Convention and the Non-European Movement. Throughout his public life, and like his father, he shied away from the ANC and eschewed confrontational politics. Similarly, Alexander juggled his editorship of *Imvo* with public activities in several organisations, including the radical Industrial Commercial Union and the Native Representative Council.

Reverend Dr Mpilo Walter Benson Rubusana. The white shirt that Rubusana, and other intellectuals of his era, wear in these photographs is significant, and signals the struggle for the heart and soul of converts carried within the colonial mission. After his baptism, Mpilo exchanged his traditional skins for a white shirt, and was given his English names in place of his Xhosa boyhood name. However, Rubusana and others like him were to reassert their identity, not only through political struggle, but through the use of indigenous languages to shape a new intellectual tradition.

5
MPILO WALTER BENSON RUBUSANA
Songezo Joel Ngqongqo

British colonialism and imperialist practices had a profoundly negative effect on the traditional life of the Xhosa in the Eastern Cape, especially during the 1840s and 1850s. The military forces of the British destroyed all surviving vestiges of independence and ended armed resistance. The survival of Xhosa independence was not helped by the infamous cattle killing instigated by the prophetess Nongqawuse.

Despite these calamities, the 1850s also produced influential African intellectuals, including Mpilo Walter Benson Rubusana. A proponent of indigenous languages, an accomplished author and journalist, and an ordained priest, Rubusana made history by becoming the first and only African to be elected onto the Cape Provincial Council.

CHILDHOOD INFLUENCES

Rubusana was born on 21 March 1858, at Mnandi, Somerset East, and given the name Mpilo. He was the eldest of ten children born to his father, Mbonjana, a farm labourer and his mother, Nomenti. Among peers and family, he was affectionately known as Nophanyaza. '*Nophanyaza*' would mean one who acts in a flash and who commands that things be done quickly. Interestingly even his father was called by such a name. Hence Rubusana was even called the son of Nophanyaza. Though illiterate, Rubusana's parents had a lasting influence on the young Mpilo. As a councillor to Chief Bhotomane of the imiDange chiefdom, his father was a custodian of African culture and languages – a path that Rubusana would later follow through his professional work.

Rubusana's early childhood gave no indications of his future successes. He spent most of his childhood herding livestock, and started school only as an adolescent, aged 16. And this happened only by chance. He was noticed by Reverend Richard Birt, who he had met while working as a stable-boy at the London Missionary Station in Peelton, near King William's Town. Birt thought he recognised a great intellectual talent in the young lad and, in 1874, enrolled him at the Boys School at Peelton's Native Training Institution.

Birt's influence on the young Rubusana paved the way for his conversion to Christianity. A year after starting at school Mpilo was baptised and given a new name: Walter Benson. His African name, Mpilo, was officially expunged, and the traditional skin he normally wore was replaced with a white shirt. This apparently marked his transition from the traditional to the modern world. For young Africans like Rubusana, embracing the white man's religion meant sacrificing a large part of their traditional identity. For instance circumcision, so important to the Xhosa in forming a young man's identity, was seen by the civilising mission as barbaric, even though it existed as a cultural ritual in many parts of the world.

MARRIAGE AND EARLY PROFESSIONAL LIFE

Upon completing formal education, the young Rubusana qualified as a teacher at Lovedale College. In 1879 he began his teaching career at Peelton. Shortly afterwards – with the encouragement of Birt – he focused his attention on his theological studies, which he pursued from 1880 to 1882.

While teaching at Peelton, Rubusana met Nomhaya Deena Nzanzana, whom he married in 1883. She was also a teacher there. They had both shared the homes of clergy in their youth – she living with the Reverend James Davidson and he with the Birts. Deena was herself extremely well educated – she had travelled to Scotland with Reverend Jameson during his sabbatical and studied at Dollar Academy, Scotland. The marriage produced twelve children, although only six

The white building in the centre used to house the old council offices in Lloyd Street, East London, and was the target of many Congress marches led by Rubusana in the first decade of the 1900s. In 1909 Rubusana became the leader of the Congress movement in the Cape. A singular achievement was being elected in 1910 as a Member of the Cape Provincial Council, representing Tembuland, a seat he lost in 1914. He was the only African ever to hold such a position. Rubusana was elected as one of the vice-presidents of the South African Native National Congress (African National Congress) when it was established in 1912.

survived to adulthood. All except one of the children became teachers. Deena passed away in 1920, and Rubusana married Bella Noni Kashe of Alice. This marriage bore one child, a son.

RUBUSANA THE EDUCATIONALIST

Rubusana started teaching at Peelton in 1879 and soon distinguished himself. But his involvement went beyond teaching and he became a committed educational activist. He found an ideological home in the Native Education Association, which confronted broad-based issues including the vote, land and pass laws. He also assisted in the establishment of more than ten schools in and around East London. Many of these schools now went as far as Standard Six. These advances in providing expanded formal education to Xhosa children were intended not only to improve their prospects of employment, but also to increase the number of black graduates qualifying for the franchise in the Cape colony.

Rubusana advocated for compulsory education, but he also went one step further than many, in advocating mother-tongue education. He believed that children had a far better chance of learning if they were instructed in their mother tongue in the early grades of school. He took to writing in Xhosa, as a way of promoting African literature, history and grammar.

AUTHOR AND JOURNALIST

Rubusana's books included *Zemk' iinkomo Magwalandini*, a book he edited, which contained praises of chiefs, missionary and traditional history and prose. This book, written in Xhosa, is set in the Eastern Cape and is a call to arms of sorts, telling of the language, history, and culture of the various Xhosa kingdoms (such as the amaGqunukwebe and Rharabe), and of Ngqika and various wars of dispossession.

He also wrote a *History of South Africa from the Native Stand Point*. He assisted with the translation of a Xhosa Bible, and filled an important void left by the death of Tiyo Soga in 1871 when he travelled to England to supervise its printing. He was also commissioned to translate prayers and other religious publications by his own and other churches on more than one occasion.

His contributions to literature and history earned him an honorary PhD from the McKinley Memorial University in Louisville, Kentucky, in the United States, in 1906.

Rubusana's journalistic involvement happened in the context of a burgeoning of African journalism in the Eastern Cape. This new form of self expression for educated Africans had grown out of missionary journalism, which no longer met the political needs of the developing middle class. Rubusana had written for *Isigidimi* and the *Christian Express* while also acting as an agent for Jabavu's paper, *Imvo Zabantsundu*, by corresponding for the newspaper, and selling it. In 1897 Rubusana and other political and civic leaders launched their own ill-fated newspaper,

Rubusana and other leaders started Izwi Labantu *in 1897 to provide African readers with an alternative to* Imvo. *Party politics of whites in the Cape Province began to influence the politics of Africans. The Cape had a liberal political system which allowed for a qualified franchise for Africans. White political parties vied for the African vote to strengthen their power in parliament.* Imvo *supported the conservative South African Party while the liberal Progressives saw fit to bankroll* Izwi *for support.*

Izwi Labantu, which was intended to give a clear voice to the political aspirations of Africans in the Eastern Cape in the late nineteenth century.

THE POLITICIAN

Rubusana had first emerged as a political leader when, together with other African leaders, he agitated against discriminatory land tenure laws. Land ownership was not only important for Africans in terms of access to productive resources, it was also an important qualification for the franchise in the Cape. A founder member of the Native Vigilance Association in the late 1880s, Rubusana was part of the very first generation of African leaders that formed political organisations to represent Africans. The shift to organised politics moved political agitation away from the personal. It was also a new and powerful threat to white-liberal agency.

Hitherto Africans in the Eastern Cape had lacked political organisation, and relied on the influential personality of John Tengo Jabavu, the towering editor of *Imvo Zabantsundu*, to speak on their behalf. Jabavu, in turn, put his faith in English-speaking liberal politicians, for whom he mobilised votes through his newspaper. He hoped that this would advance the cause of Africans in parliament. Known as 'friends of the natives', the liberals later turned against native voters and supported legislation that introduced restrictions designed to limit the number of eligible African voters. Jabavu continued to support them nonetheless. Rubusana and his peers felt betrayed by Jabavu. They attributed Jabavu's complicity to his indebtedness to the liberals for having financed his newspaper. As a result, Rubusana became part of the initiative that formed a rival newspaper, *Izwi Labantu*, in 1897. The title, 'The Voice of the People', denoted a forceful and militant approach to issues, quite different to Jabavu's moderately titled newspaper, 'Native Opinion' (*Imvo Zabantsundu*).

If Jabavu had been the officially recognised spokesperson for Africans in the Cape, Rubusana had become their popular leader and organiser. As his political involvement grew, he was elected president of the Cape-based Native Congress, which had grown in strength in the 1880s and 1890s. When the provincial Congresses merged to form the South African Native Convention in 1909, Rubusana was elected

The Twins' Return.

It is my pleasant duty to extend to Mr. Sauer and Mr. Merriman a cordial welcome back to South Africa. At present there are only two places of residence which they are inclined to take up, the good old Home Country and our own miserable and wretched part of the world. As one therefore has only two places to choose from, I am perfectly logical in expressing joy that our own land is again to be favoured in preference to England. Of two evils one must choose the lesser, and all things considered Mr. Merriman and Mr. Sauer are decidedly lesser evils here than in the Homeland. If it were possible to permanently locate them at Brussels, Berlin, or even Robben Island, one would be content, but for the present no such prospect is open.

I do not find very much result from the campaign of mendacity these worthies have been waging during their tour, but there was always a danger that they might do a little harm. The intelligent British public cannot know Mr. Sauer and Mr. Merriman as we know them. They know them only as public men and ex-Ministers, and despite recent study of South African questions, they have never quite got rid of the traditional idea that ex-Ministers are at least decent and honourable members of society. The British public assumes them to be at least fairly truthful, and fairly courteous and possessed of a tolerable knowledge of the nature of an oath. They cannot realise the Minister who, after swearing allegiance to a Sovereign and whilst holding office under His representative, intrigues with that Sovereign's enemies and thwarts and maligns that Sovereign's High Commissioner. They assume that if a Minister held sentiments leading him to such things, he would be sufficiently honourable to openly disavow his allegiance and to resign his office. So the British public attach some little credence to men with Ministerial antecedents, whereas we, who know what things Ministers can be and can do and have done, believe in nothing. For us the return of the political twins has no terrors. Whatever harm may be done, they will contribute little to it. An Ishmael and a Judas do not constitute a partnership likely to gather much following around them, and the names of Mr. Merriman and Mr. Sauer are so well known in this Colony as to suffice to drive away from the "South African" Party not a few who might otherwise join themselves to it. It is no exaggeration to say that in our Parliament no member is disliked as Mr. Merriman is disliked, no member mistrusted as Mr. Sauer is mistrusted. Party spirit is not responsible for this to any great extent. For the great bulk of men on the other side the Progressive members entertain respect, or at least pity, but in the case of these worthies the purely personal factor comes in, and causes them to be regarded with exactly the same feelings as would be their lot were they met with in any other sphere than that of politics, and a deeper Inferno than this could scarcely be imagined. Indeed it is questionable whether they are held in any more personal esteem on their own side, and nothing could show more clearly the paucity of able men in the seditious party than their selection for the posts of envoys to the people of England.

In this connection it is most instructive to note the failure of the Afrikander, astute though he is in most things, when the strategy of high politics should come into play. Throughout this whole controversy, our opponents, most fortunately, have done exactly what we could have wished them to do. From Kruger downwards through all the hierarchy of rebellion, they have consistently done their best to prove our case. It is no different to Mr. Chamberlain's reputation to say that they have placed better works at his disposal than he has created.

Mrs. CLEGG'S
Established Registry for Servants & Situations.
11, CHURCH STREET, CAPE TOWN.

for himself, and in no instance did they play into our hands more effectively than when they put up Mr. Sauer and Mr. Merriman as their chief spokesmen in the House of Assembly last year. I have before pointed out that it would have been perfectly possible for the disloyalists to have been fairly successful in concealing their disloyalty, had they adopted the plan of putting up level-headed men to attack only selected portions of the Government procedure; to have argued, for instance, temperately against the policy of war whilst carefully avoiding any attacks on the British army or revealing any brief they held in defence of rebellion. But men like the twins in question are nothing if not combative, scurrilous and vindictive, and they succeeded in leaving the whole world with nothing but their bare assertion of loyalty to put against the evidence, of almost every word they spoke, that they and their Party were disloyal to the core. And they can all this by sending the very men who had so effectively damaged the idol of Bondism here, to complete the task of disabusing the British Public of the last shred of belief in the pro-Boer cult. We take off our hats to them, we take off our hats to Kruger for uniting the British Empire. It is well that they went to England. Without them it is just possible, altruistic as the British public is, that some remnant of the edifice of sympathy with the vanishing Boer might have remained. And it is well that they have come back. There is much for them to do here. The honest decent-minded Dutch farmer requires showing that he is led by the nose by a set of the blackest political charlatans that ever disgraced this earth. The Mugwumps want showing even yet what political Afrikanderism really is. No one can perform this enlightening work better than the two returning wanderers, the champion smashers of every cause with which they were ever allied.

The New Pavilion.—Mr. B. Goodman presents his patrons this week with a particularly good programme...

The Gaiety Company.—The Gaiety Musical Comedy Company's latest production, "A Runaway Girl,"...

FOR WINTER WEAR.—Overcoats, Waterproofs, Waistcoats. Latest Shapes and Patterns.—**HATCH, Shortmarket Street.**

BUY
EUREKA WATERPROOFS.
EVERY GARMENT GUARANTEED.
Obtainable all over South Africa.

The Native Question.

To the Editor of the SOUTH AFRICAN REVIEW.

Sir,—Having had special facilities for watching your attitude towards the Native Question as it invariably presents itself to the European public, I feel impelled to write to you and offer my sincerest congratulations on the clear, manly, and outspoken manner in which you continue to deal with the vexed questions that arise, and the firm grasp and fair-minded presentations of wholesome views and opinions that appear in your paper regarding the same.

I take up the position, so well put by you, that a medium course is the best, and that extreme, as you say, "of talking about the Kafir as if he were a nuisance and a potential slave, or of pampering him up as if he were a hot-house plant," must always be avoided. That must form the standard or fundamental principle of his treatment by the European public, and of his government by his rulers; any other course is not only unjust but is likely to prove disastrous in the long run to the amicable relations and the permanent peace and security of His Majesty's lieges. But I would go further and endeavour to dispel the fallacy that the native is discontented with his race or colour and aspires to become a European. There is nothing in his conduct to justify this implication, for, in his pride of race, he has not forgotten in the past to comport himself with the dignity and indifference to European women that is remarkable in those who are far too frequently looked upon as savages. If there is any deterioration in his manners of which we hear complaints in the streets and side-walks, the fault must be attributed to the influence of association or contact with the bad manners, degraded habits, and social vices which are copied from those who plume themselves on their superior civilization and which were foreign to him in his tribal state. However his laws as to treatment of females may be criticised, his conduct towards that sex was not devoid of chivalry, nor was it countenanced by his customs or his chief. It is a mistake to think that the heathen Kafir was no gentleman, and even now in his transitory state, with all its drawbacks and temptations, those dreadful assaults or bestial crimes on European or any other class of females which are so frequent in other countries, are, it must be admitted, remarkable by their absence. This I think any fair-minded Englishman will be ready to concede, although, unfortunately, ordinary colonial opinion is inclined to slander them in this respect. Can we say this with equal assurance of his more civilized white neighbour towards coloured women? The scenes daily enacted in Capo Town, and in fact throughout the country amongst white men of all classes, point to a most degraded moral standard unworthy of the civilization and superiority of which they pride themselves in an offensive way when speaking of the aborigines.

Let us put away cant and face the question in its proper relations to this everlasting coloured crusade, for where the sexes are concerned it disappears only to re-appear, with more obstinacy, amongst the males. The inference is obvious. Therefore the males (amongst natives) and you have a solution of the coloured question, and obliterate the line of cleavage. Of course such a solution is impossible and absurd, for whatever the English-man's susceptibilities about his own women may be, or his desire to monopolize the coloured women also as a perquisite of his race, he will eventually find that he has taken up an impossible position.—I am, etc.,

(Rev.) W. B. RUBUSANA,
Native Missionary.
East London, June 19th, 1901.

F. L. BISHOP,
BROKER, ESTATE AND GENERAL AGENT,
8, National Bank Chambers, St. George's St.

A letter to the South African Review, 1901. Styling himself a 'native missionary', Rubusana voiced strong ideas about racial issues and the behaviour of all races in the colony towards women.

president of the nation-wide body, confirming his stature and popularity as a national leader.

In that same year, the African electorate in the Cape elected him to the Cape Provincial Council. He became their official spokesperson and the first-ever African political representative in the history of electoral politics in the Cape.

As an official representative of his people, Rubusana was a member of numerous delegations to England to petition the British government. He lobbied, though unsuccessfully, to advance the political aspirations of black people in South Africa. In 1910, as white South Africa moved towards union, he and other leaders urged Africans to unite. The culmination of this unification drive was the launching of the South African Native National Congress in Bloemfontein in 1912.

Unfortunately, Jabavu's response to Rubusana's new status created tensions which were ultimately to explode in the face of the black electorate. Jabavu was not pleased to see his leadership role taken over by Rubusana. In 1914, Jabavu challenged Rubusana for his seat, thus forcing African voters to choose between them. Inevitably the black vote split. Rubusana garnered 852 to Jabavu's 294 votes. Even though Rubusana had more votes than Jabavu, he still fell short of a majority. The seat went to a white candidate, who was supported by an undivided block of white voters.

ONGOING RIVALRY

In many ways this personal rivalry also reflected a denominational rivalry that Rubusana had tried hard to avoid. On several occasions, Jabavu's Wesleyans and Rubusana's Congregationalists were pitted against one another. Some of the disputes were over land on which to build churches or schools. Rubusana had tried hard to eschew denominational conflict. The schools he helped set up, for instance, were not affiliated to any denomination. He disapproved of this conflict, reasoning that it added yet another dividing line within a community that was already fraught with divisions along class, ethnic and political

The tombstone on Rubusana's grave in East London. Born in 1858, Rubusana died in 1936, aged 78, at Frere Hospital in East London. His funeral was the biggest ever seen in East London and was attended by national political leaders and church dignatories, as well as thousands of mourners who assembled on the street lining the road to the cemetery to give thanks for the life and achievements of this extraordinary man. Rubusana's fame as a political leader should not eclipse the fact that he was also an intellectual, linguist, writer and journalist. Rubusana was also active in the church and in education and had championed the establishment of schools and churches in the Eastern Cape, particularly the East London area.

lines. Rubusana opposed denominational divisions even in his priesthood. Ordained on 25 March, 1885, he actively sought to use the offices of the church and church-related structures, such as the Independent Order of the True Templars, to unite the broader African community, thus breaking with the denominational movement. This opposition stemmed from nationalist orientation. Denominational affiliation was one of many obstacles in the way of Africans presenting a common front against colonial subjugation. Despite Rubusana's efforts, the denominational rivalry ultimately turned into a personal rivalry between himself and Jabavu.

The rivalry extended to educational matters as well. Both leaders aspired to establish a college for Africans, but differed on their choice of location. Jabavu preferred Alice, while Rubusana favoured Queenstown as a suitable site for their planned endeavour. Jabavu, with white financial assistance, eventually prevailed. This victory gave birth in 1916 to what is now known as the University of Fort Hare.

WITHDRAWAL FROM PUBLIC LIFE

Rubusana's influence in black politics waned in the face of the radicalisation of African workers and the ascendancy of the Communist Party of South Africa (founded in 1919) and the trade-union movement of the inter-war years. Rubusana's attempt to re-capture his seat in 1920 failed, making his short parliamentary tenure the first and only by an African in Cape politics.

Thereafter, he gradually withdrew from public life, and eventually passed away on 19 April 1936. His legacy lives not only in memory, but still is visible in the numerous schools and churches he set up in the area of East London. Almost all of these schools and churches were demolished during the apartheid programme of forced removal in the 1960s and 1970s, when thousands of African inhabitants of East London were uprooted to Mdantsane, a township in the Ciskei homeland, thirty miles away.

6

SAMUEL EDWARD KRUNE MQHAYI

Mncedisi Qangule

A renowned poet and author, Mqhayi embodied the transition of African narratives from the oral tradition to the written word. He fused his natural talent for oratory and story-telling with his literary training to produce the first ever literary collection by an *imbongi* – a poet and keeper of history.

Samuel Edward Krune Mqhayi was born on 1 December 1875, at the village of Gcumashe, on the banks of the Thyume River. His birth came as an answer to his parents' regular prayers for a boy child. They gave him the biblical name, Samuel, as they saw him as a gift from God.

CHILDHOOD INFLUENCES

By the close of the nineteenth century, the civilising mission had begun to bear fruit throughout the Eastern Cape. The first crop of African intellectuals influenced by the missions had begun writing and publishing works, and these reached the Thyume area where Mqhayi was born. Thus, the young Mqhayi had personal encounters with, and was exposed to the works of, influential figures such as John Tengo Jabavu. In fact, his schoolmaster, Reverend Makhiwane, was an author and literary figure himself and took a personal interest in the young Mqhayi.

As a child, Mqhayi appears to have been enthralled by the richness of indigenous history. Tradition has it that he was an avid listener to fireside *amabali* (tales told of long ago). He showed a natural talent for oratory from early on.

Samuel Edward Krune Mqhayi (1875–1945) was a famed imbongi. He fused Xhosa orality with western poetic structures to create a new hybrid Xhosa poetry. He was also a keeper of history and culture, in both his published works and his position as praise singer to Chief Ndlambe.

MQHAYI, THE IMBONGI

Mqhayi wrote extensively, both poetry and prose, and dealt with a wide variety of subjects. He often wrote of history and abstract ideas such as truth, hope and love, using the morality of his time as the foundation stone for constructing a revitalised African morality. He particularly excelled in traditional heroic poetry, and demonstrated great skill in weaving his people's customs, legends and myths into his poems. He had an intimate knowledge of Xhosa traditions and customs, which he gained through association with and service to royalty. His work reflects this rich and varied knowledge.

Mqhayi was, however, no ordinary *imbongi*. He redefined the scope and the subject matter of an *imbongi*. Previously, *iimbongi* were focused inwardly on their societies. In this role they would praise or criticise the power structure to highlight abuses of power. They would also be generally concerned with the morality and welfare of the populace. Mqhayi, however, went a step further: he modified and enlarged this poetic tradition by including whites as poetic subjects.

This change of subject came about as a result of Mqayi's perception of the political changes he saw happening in the Eastern Cape. He saw the subjugation of Africans, as power began to concentrate in white hands in the Eastern Cape. Adapting and expanding the traditional role played by an *imbongi* in response to these powerful historical forces, Mqhayi created praise poetry of exceptional quality.

MQHAYI'S CONTRIBUTION TO XHOSA PRAISE POETRY

His genius was further illustrated in his adaptation of Xhosa praise poetry to European style and strictures. There were hurdles associated with this shift, which his work exposes. In some poems, he struggled to maintain balance and unity. The rhyme scheme is discernibly the major problem. Good rhyme, in any poem, creates free flow and a unifying musicality. Static or forced rhyme spoils the integrity of the rhythm and the unity or wholeness in the poem. In the poem *Umsintsi*,

The tree under which Mqhayi would sit during an imbizo *of the elders. What inspired him most were the lives of rural dwellers who would sit under* umthombe *(trees) such as these, enjoying stories about the past and present.*

for instance, Mqhayi struggles to maintain balance through rhyme. In English, rhyme is realised by the repetition of the last syllable of the line. As it is difficult to find such meaningful rhyming words in Xhosa, adopting the western style becomes even more difficult.

In other languages, such as English, a tradition has been established regarding the use of rhyme. The difficulty that Mqhayi experiences can also be felt in the following lines:

Okwenene ngumthi om__hle__
Onkonzo zobomvu zin__hle__
Ngumthi wohlobo lomd__ubu__
Ochuma utsho ngezid__umba__

The underlined syllables in the extract above do not rhyme properly. When rhyme is forced, artistry is lost through artificiality.

However, the poem entitled *'Isimo somhlaba'* can be singled out as a major breakthrough in the use of rhyme by a Xhosa poet. There is a marked improvement in the use of this device. The surface structure of the poem also complements the deep structure. This feature, together with the rhyming scheme, forms a pattern that creates balance and unity in the poem. There is no fragmentation of the chain of ideas that permeates the poem and a feeling of self-discipline pervades. Mqhayi also uses an interesting line pattern to great effect. The long and short lines in this extract are an example of this:

ndihlangene neentwazana
ndisiya komkhulu
zazintle ezo ntwazana
zazintle kakhulu

This is in stark contrast to Xhosa praise poetry, which takes neither the length of line nor rhythm into consideration.

Xhosa praise poetry is free from all the restrictions that characterise English or Afrikaans poetry. However, Mqhayi's success in the applica-

A family member shows the remnants of the foundation of the Mqhayi house in Tyotyora, where Mqhayi grew up. As a child the young Mqhayi would have herded cattle, and apparently would often break into spontaneous praise eulogising his favourite livestock and his childhood friends. Later his works would reach beyond the confines of his traditional village.

Chief Makinana at his village, Berlin, near King William's Town. He is a descendant of Chief Ndlambe, to whom Mqhayi was imbongi

tion of new techniques in Xhosa poetry shows that one cannot jump to the conclusion that Xhosa poetry is inflexible. A skilled approach to the employment of western techniques can result in a successful new form of Xhosa poetry. An interesting line of research would be to investigate to what extent poets who followed Mqhayi have pursued the incorporation of western ideas into their own works, and to assess to what degree it has been successful.

MQHAYI THE AUTHOR

Mqhayi made his debut as an author in 1914 with the publication of *Ityala lamawele* (*The lawsuit of the twins*). The book went on to become one of the most cited texts in Xhosa literature, casting him in the same light as that doyen of Xhosa literature, Dr Mpilo Walter Benson Rubusana. In that text, Mqhayi examined the role and execution of justice. In his view, justice and law formed the bedrock on which the foundations of social order are laid. He set his text in a pre-colonial context, paying particular attention to these questions: firstly, how law was interpreted formally whenever there was a civil or criminal dispute between two or more people; and secondly, what the nature and operation of law was in Xhosa traditional and indigenous society.

A number of other themes are easily identifiable in Mqhayi's works. These themes tend to overlap in his publications, and some themes become more dominant than others. For instance, *Don Jadu* (1929) is on disunity and lack of socio-political advancement among blacks. Here Mqhayi expresses a concern about the well-being of the Xhosa people in particular and all the other black people in southern Africa in general. He felt that in the same way in which the British and German nations achieved unity, the Xhosa, Zulus, Sothos and Tswanas should unite to form one big *ntu*, or nation. It is clear in this text that Mqhayi is one of those writers who could not remain silent in the face of an injustice. He suggests, in a rather subtle manner, that the erosion of the dignity of a black person by any factor or element will be put to an end by a united black force.

But Mqhayi did not advocate that blacks put political and economic power towards the destruction of the white presence among them. On the contrary, he pleaded for racial co-operation, counselling that whites could become agents for good. To illustrate this point, he uses

Samuel

This is now the name of the author of this paper. He was born in the Chumie valley at that old Mission station known as Gqumahashe.[4] It is said that it was in the hoeing season for the women threw down their hoes to go and attend his mother giving birth to a child. This was on the 1st December, 1875. The women of the village made much of their duty as midwives, because it was the first male child born to my father, and moreover, my father was the best educated man in that area. The poet sums up the whole rejoicing in the following lines:

What is this movement,
Among men and mothers?
[What is this excitement about?]
As if it is for a time of merriment?
Ziwani's wife has given birth
The village is full of joy.

Horses are running about,
To-day in this Gqumaha∫e;
Even hoes are thrown away,
The message is startling;
Ziwani's wife has given birth
To-day she is delivered of a bold one.

Shall we rejoice, or be anxious?
Are we to be happy, or to hope?
We have often given birth to children,
To maidens or to lads.
This day Nomenti is delivered of a child,
She wept for this little one.

Let us rejoice with her,
For we wept with her,
Her petition has been received;
Her groaning has been answered,
She has been delivered of a son,
And she said he is equal to ten sons.

Hail thou, with the little one.
So say we the same to you, young man.
Although we are lacking in presents,
Lacking in words suitable for prayers;
Health to you child of Bedle.

[This day, yes, we have gained]
For we asked of the Creator,
This man appeared through petitions.
And his name is "asked for" (Samuel).
Ziwani's wife has given birth --
The Lord is gracious.

Petitions are answered;
Trials are dissipated;
Lift up your hearts,
With the "I Am" there is listening
To the groanings and petitions
He has caused the heart to rejoice.

We pray for the young man,
And to the "I Am" we give thanks to,
Would He would preserve the lad
From things that come knocking,
That seek to surround him,
And prevent his succeeding.

We say it of wars and beer-gatherings;
We say it of poverty and famine;
We say it of pride and envy;
And of being lifted up in honour;
May he never be drawn to evil gain;
And that until he has wrinkles.

Therefore we expect him to be preserved;
We ask for all gifts for him;
For those of the earth and heaven
For those of the deep unto deep
[And he be some help to the race]
To be a strength unto the race.

Amen.

Mqhayi was a much loved child, as this poem about his birth attests.

the biblical analogy of a spear that, even though it is a lethal weapon, can also be turned into a life-sustaining plough.

In *Inzuzo* (1943) Mqhayi casts an incisive eye on patriotism, while in *uMqhayi wase Ntabozuko* he illustrates the making of a man. Mqhayi's many texts reveal an intense interest in a variety of social issues.

MQHAYI THE EDUCATOR AND HISTORIAN

An educator by training, Mqhayi was highly critical of (colonial) education, even though he was a product of it. He credited colonial education for the benefits of civilisation, but was also aware that it was attuned to advance the selfish interests of colonialism and European imperialism.

Mqhayi observed:

> *Ukuhamba behlolela iinkosi zabo ezibahlawulayo umhlaba.*
> *Bahamba nalo ilizwi ukuba lihamba liba yingcambane*
> *yokulawula izikhumbani nesizwe, yathi imfuno yayinto nje*
> *eyenzelwe ukuba kuviwane ngentetho.*

> Human movement in search of land grabbing land from chiefs,
> Using the word of God as a tool
> And instrument to rule Kings and nations
> An education so inferior
> Became an institution to prepare slaves for new masters
> – translation by MP Qanqubi

The teaching of black history was also given some attention by Mqhayi. History, he contends, is not the mere recording of events. It must capture and present in acceptable form the cumulative experiences of humankind. This viewpoint emerged in a series of biographies he wrote on leading African personalities. These included one on Simon Phamotse, teacher and founder of *Naledi ea Basotho* (The Star of Lesotho). Mqhayi singled him out for particular praise for the way he strove to create good relationships between his country and other countries in southern Africa. He held up Tshaka, Mlanjeni and Reverend Tiyo Soga as the pride of black people – icons whose achievements should be emulated by future generations. They owed this distinction to their determination, diligence, and the sacrifices they made so that their people could gain recognition in the world. The biographies he wrote of these men, however, cannot be compared to his own autobiography and his biography of John Knox Bokwe, in terms of depth of research. They are nevertheless a recommendable account of relevant historical facts and valuable information.

MQHAYI'S LEGACY

Mqhayi's historical relevance as an *imbongi* is beyond doubt. He is seen as a repository of his people's history, culture, tradition and customs. His experience as an historian and a traditional bard, living close to many chiefs, made that possible.

As a pioneer of indigenous languages, Mqhayi had a special interest in African thought and as a linguist he embarked on standardising Xhosa grammar. As a distinguished scholar, he devoted himself mainly to progressive writing. He was also an apostle of change, and a patriot.

Perhaps above all, Mqhayi will forever be remembered as a protest poet who stoked the fires of nationalist resistance. Nelson Mandela recalls his first encounter with Mqhayi while at school as a truly inspirational moment:

> ... the sight of a black man in tribal dress coming through that door was electrifying. It is hard to explain the impact it had on us. It seemed to turn the universe upside down ... he raised his assegai into the air for emphasis, and accidentally hit the curtain above him ... he ... faced us, and newly energised, exclaimed that this incident – the assegai striking the wire – symbolised the clash between the culture of Africa and that of Europe. His voice rose and he said: 'The assegai stands for what is glorious and true in African history; it is a symbol of the African as warrior and the African as artist. This metal wire,' he said, pointing above, 'is an example of Western manufacturing, which is skilful but cold, clever but soulless. ... what I am talking to you about is the brutal clash between what is indigenous and good, and what is foreign and

Mqhayi's grave near Berlin in the Eastern Cape. A noted Xhosa historian and novelist, Mqhayi's biographical writings record the lives of famous South Africans such as Tshaka, Mlanjeni, Tiyo Soga and John Knox Bokwe. His novels criticise, both directly and indirectly, the racist direction of the colonial British state of the time, and articulate a new nationalism.

bad. We cannot allow these foreigners who do not care for our culture to take over our nation. I predict that, one day, the forces of African society will achieve a momentous victory over the interloper. For too long we have succumbed to the false gods of the white man. But we shall emerge and cast off these foreign notions.'

I could hardly believe my ears. His boldness in speaking of such delicate matters in the presence of Dr Wellington and other whites seemed utterly astonishing to us. Yet at the same time it aroused and motivated us, and began to alter my perception of men like Dr Wellington, who I had automatically considered my benefactor.

NOTES

This book is intended to be a popular history that we hope will be widely read by those interested in South African heritage and history. We have therefore kept notes and sources to a minimum. However, to acknowledge our obligation to academic discipline and our indebtedness to our source material, we have provided these 'silent' notes instead of adding citations to the text.

1. INTRODUCTION

page	line	
1	17	Suttner 2005
2	3	Du Plessis 1910: 404
2	10	Roux 1966
3	3	Cook 1949: 350
3	23	Mostert 1992
4	6	Mostert 1992
4	19	Bundy 1979: 39
5	3	Trapido 1980

2. NTSIKANA

page	line	
7	22	Bokwe 1914
9	11	Jordan cited in Gerard 1971
9	26	Bokwe 1914: 8
10	10	Ntsikana cited in Bennie (undated): 9–10
10	30	Jordan cited in Gerard 1971: 27
11	5	Bokwe 1914: 17
12	10	Soga cited in Bennie (undated): 5
13	9	Bokwe 1914: 23
13	19	Bokwe 1914: 24
13	25	Bokwe 1914: 26
15	3	Bokwe 1914: 20

| 15 | 11 | Bokwe 1914: 20 |
| 15 | 22 | Bokwe 1914: 18 |

3. TIYO SOGA

page	line	
17	23	Cousins 1897
19	3	Chalmers 1877
20	17	Chalmers 1877: 58
21	2	Williams 1978
21	9	Chalmers 1877: 85-86
21	20	Soga cited in Chalmers 1877: 75
21	33	Chalmers 1877: 136
23	8	Chalmers 1877: 132
24	3	Chalmers 1877: 290
25	9	Chalmers 1877: 136
25	14	Chalmers 1877: 136
26	20	Chalmers 1877: 314
27	2	Chalmers 1877: 431
27	5	Chalmers 1877: 338
27	27	Chalmers 1877: 359–360
28	5	Williams 1978
28	23	Chalmers 1877: 433–434
29	3	Chalmers 1877: 430
29	14	Chalmers, 1877: 314

4. JOHN TENGO JABAVU

page	line	
31	13	Jabavu 1922
33	5	Jabavu 1922
34	17	Roux 1966
35	13	Roux 1966
35	23	Trapido 1980
35	33	Trapido 1980
37	13	Ngcongco 1970
39	20	Trapido 1980
40	6	Plaatje 1916

40	24	Plaatje 1916: 196
42	13	Mqingwana 1982

5. MPILO WALTER BENSON RUBUSANA

page	line	
46	14	*Christian Express*, 1-12-1905
48	24	Briggs and Wing 1970
50	last line	Ngcongco 1971
54	16	Odendaal 1984
54	28	Ngqongqo 1996
54	22	Gerhart and Karis 1977

6. SAMUEL EDWARD NKRUNE MQHAYI

page	line	
55	10	Mqhayi 1939
58	4	Mqhayi 1943
58	11	*Umthetheli wa-Bantu* 07-01-1928
59	11	*Umthetheli wa-Bantu* 07-01-1928, 28-02-1931
63	17	Mqhayi 1943
64	8	Mqhayi 1939
65	11	Mandela 1994: 39

PICTURE CREDITS

p 8 from John Knox Bokwe (1914) *Ntsikana: The Story of an African Convert.* Lovedale: Lovedale Press

pp 16 & 24 from Donovan Williams (1978) *Umfundisi: A Biography of Tiyo Soga, 1829–1871.* Lovedale: Lovedale Press

pp 12, 14, 22, 29, 34, 47, 58, 59, 60, 65 by Ashwell Adriaan

pp 19 & 33 used with kind permission of the Cory Library, Rhodes University, Grahamstown

pp 32, 42 used with kind permission of the Jababvu Family Archive

pp 36, 38, 49, 51, 62 supplied by the South African National Library, Cape Town

p 44 used with kind permission of Amathole Museum, King William's Town

p 56 Taken from Patricia E Scott (1976) *Samuel Edward Krune Mqhayi, 1875–1945, Communication 5,* Department of African Languages, Rhodes University, Grahamstown

The authors gratefully acknowledge the picture research done by Ashwell Adriaan, and the help of the Amathole Museum in King William's Town in sourcing the photographs used in this book. We also thank Didier Jonkers for his skillful scanning and retouching. Every effort was made to trace the copyright holders but, in some instances, this was not possible. The publishers would be grateful for further information and will make appropriate arrangements in relation to this.

CONTRIBUTORS

Vuyani Booi
An MA graduate in Public and Visual History from the University of the Western Cape, Booi is a heritage specialist and works at the National Heritage and Cultural Studies Centre, Fort Hare University, Alice.

Mcebisi Ndletyana
Ndletyana holds a PhD in Political Science from the University of the Witwatersrand. He is a Senior Research Specialist at the Democracy and Governance Research Program, Human Sciences Research Council.

Songezo Joel Ngqongqo
A historian with an MA degree from Fort Hare University, Songezo is a biographer of WBM Rubusana.

Mncedisi Qangule
An oral poet and author, Mncedisi has an Honours degree in Literature from Ibadan University, Nigeria.

REFERENCES

Bennie WG (Undated) *Imibengo*. Alice: Lovedale Press
Bokwe JK (1914) *Ntsikana: The story of an African convert*. Alice: Lovedale Press
Briggs DR and Wing J (1970) *The harvest and the hope: The story of Congregationalism in Southern Africa*. Johannesburg: United Congregational Church of Southern Africa
Bundy C (1979) *The rise and fall of the South African peasantry*. Cape Town: David Phillip
Chalmers JA (1877) *Tiyo Soga: A page of South African mission work*. Edinburgh: Andrew Elliot
Cook PA (1949) Non-European education. In E Hellmann (Ed.) *Handbook on race-relations in South Africa*. London: Oxford University Press
Cousins HT (1897) *Tiyo Soga: The model kafir missionary*. London: SW Partridge and Co.
Du Plessis J (1910) *A history of Christian missions in South Africa*. London: Struik
Gerard AS (1971) *Four African literatures: Xhosa, Sotho, Zulu, Amharic*. Berkeley: University of California Press
Gerhart GM and Karis T (1977) *From protest to challenge: A documentary history of African politics in South Africa 1882–1964*. Vol. 4. California: Hoover Institution Press
Jabavu DDT (1922) *The life of John Tengo Jabavu: Editor of Imvo Zabantsundu, 1884–1921*. Alice: Lovedale Press
Mandela N (1994) *Long Walk to Freedom: The Autobiography of Nelson Mandela*. Johannesburg: Macdonald Purnell
Mostert N (1992) *Frontiers: The epic of South Africa's creation and the tragedy of the Xhosa people*. New York: Alfred Knopf
Mqhayi SEK (1914) *Ityala Lamawele*. Alice: Lovedale Press
Mqhayi SEK (1929) *The First Xhosa Utopia – U-Don Jadu*. Alice: Lovedale Press
Mqhayi SEK (1939) *U-Mqhayi wase Ntab' Uzuko*. Alice: Lovedale Press
Mqhayi SEK (1943) *Inzuzo*. Alice: Lovedale Press

Mqingwana GV (1982) John Tengo Jabavu and the South African Native College. *Annals of the Grahamstown Historical Society* Vol. 3 Issue 4

Ngcongco LD (1970) Jabavu and the Anglo-Boer War. *Kleio* Vol. 2 Issue 2

Ngcongco LD (1971) John Tengo Jabavu, 1859–1921. In C Saunders (Ed.) *Black leaders in Southern African history*. London: Heinemann

Ngqongqo SJ (1996) Mpilo Walter Benson Rubusana 1858–1910: The making of the new African elite in the Eastern Cape. MA thesis, University of Fort Hare

Odendaal A (1984) *Vukani Bantu: The beginnings of black protest politics in South Africa to 1912*. Cape Town: David Philip

Plaatje TS (1916) *Native life in South Africa*. Braamfontein: Ravan Press

Roux E (1966) *Time longer than rope*. Madison: University of Wisconsin

Soga JH (1930) *The South Eastern Bantu*. Johannesburg: Witwatersrand University Press

Suttner R (2005) The character and formation of intellectuals within the ANC-led South African liberation movement. In T Mkandawire (Ed.) *African Intellectuals*. London: Zed Books

Trapido S (1980) Friends of the natives. In S Marks (Ed.) *Economy and society in pre-industrial South Africa*. London: Longman Group

Williams D (1978) *Umfundisi: A biography of Tiyo Soga, 1829–1871*. Alice: Lovedale Press